Social Policy for an Aging Society

Carole B. Cox, MSW, PhD, is professor at the Graduate School of Social Service, Fordham University. She is a fellow of the Gerontological Society of America and a Fulbright scholar. She is the author of more than 50 journal articles and chapters dealing with various aspects of aging and caregiving, with extensive research on caregivers for persons with dementia, their needs, and their use of services. Her recent work includes a study of the impact of dementia on the workplace. Her caregiving research also includes that of grandparents raising grandchildren, leading to the development of a curriculum, *Empowering Grandparents Raising Grandchildren: A Training Manual for Group Leaders* (Springer Publishing Company, 2000). She is the editor of *To Grandmother's House We Go and Stay: Perspectives on Custodial Grandparents* (Springer Publishing Company, 2000). Her other books include *Home Care for the Elderly: An International Perspective*, coauthored with Abraham Monk (1991); *The Frail Elderly: Problems, Needs, and Community Responses* (1993); *Ethnicity and Social Work Practice*, coauthored with Paul Ephross (1998); *Community Care for an Aging Society: Policies and Services* (Springer Publishing Company, 2005); and *Dementia and Social Work Practice* (Springer Publishing Company, 2007).

Social Policy for an Aging Society

A Human Rights Perspective

Carole B. Cox, MSW, PhD

SPRINGER PUBLISHING COMPANY

NEW YORK

Springer Publishing Company, LLC
11 West 42nd Street
New York, NY 10036
www.springerpub.com

Acquisitions Editor: Sheri W. Sussman
Composition: MPS Ltd.

ISBN: 978-0-8261-9653-8
e-book ISBN: 978-0-8261-9656-9

15 16 17 18 / 5 4 3 2 1

The author and the publisher of this Work have made every effort to use sources
believed to be reliable to provide information that is accurate and compatible with the
standards generally accepted at the time of publication. The author and publisher shall
not be liable for any special, consequential, or exemplary damages resulting, in whole
or in part, from the readers' use of, or reliance on, the information contained in this
book. The publisher has no responsibility for the persistence or accuracy of URLs for
external or third-party Internet websites referred to in this publication and does not
guarantee that any content on such websites is, or will remain, accurate or appropriate.

Library of Congress Cataloging-in-Publication Data

CIP data is available from the Library of Congress.

Special discounts on bulk quantities of our books are available to corporations,
professional associations, pharmaceutical companies, health care organizations, and
other qualifying groups. If you are interested in a custom book, including chapters
from more than one of our titles, we can provide that service as well.

For details, please contact:
Special Sales Department, Springer Publishing Company, LLC
11 West 42nd Street, 15th Floor, New York, NY 10036-8002
Phone: 877-687-7476 or 212-431-4370; Fax: 212-941-7842
E-mail: sales@springerpub.com

Printed in the United States of America by Gasch Printing.

This book is dedicated to Eleanor Roosevelt, for her humanity, spirit, and vision for a socially just world; to all of us who are aging; and to Juliana and Emilia, who have just begun.

Contents

Preface

The world is aging and, with any luck, so are we. Declining birth rates and longer life spans are contributing to the rapid growth of the older population. According to the United Nations, the global population of those 65 and older is expected to triple to 1.5 billion by 2050 with, for the first time, people 65 and over outnumbering children under age 5. The issues evoked by an aging world pose new challenges with regard to employment, health, retirement, families, and the economy. Societies respond to these challenges in varying ways and these responses can be subsumed under the rubric of social policies. Such policies tend to reflect cultural values and attitudes toward aging and the roles and responsibilities of older adults and governments in addressing aging issues.

As well as reflecting underlying perceptions of aging, policies can also influence them. To the extent that aging is perceived as a problem with people having increasing needs that drain a country's resources, older adults are vulnerable to discrimination. From this deficit perspective, aging itself is a problem and the role of policy is to meet the many needs of a dependent population. At the same time, as this perspective marginalizes and discriminates against older adults, it impedes their ability to participate in society and to remain productive and independent.

The alternative perspective of aging policy presented in this book perceives the challenges associated with aging as opportunities for developing policies that are based on the realization of human rights rather than meeting needs. Such policies perceive older adults as creators of social capital that can be used to benefit both themselves and others. Whereas a needs-based approach further discriminates against older adults, a rights-based approach acts to foster full integration.

Human rights apply to everyone; they do not diminish with age. When age is used as a proxy for competency and functional well-being, many aspects of a person's life are threatened, including the basic rights of independence, security, and dignity. Moreover, impairment itself does not diminish the importance of these rights or of the role of policies in ensuring they are met. Thus, even those with chronic conditions that impede functioning share the same basic rights free of discrimination.

This book has evolved out of my own interest in social policy and its relationship to older adults. My first policy book used a needs-based approach, *The Frail Elderly: Problems, Needs, and Community Responses* (Auburn House, 1993), whereas my second policy book, *Community Care for an Aging Society*, focused on the concerns of older adults living in the community and services that could foster their independence (Springer Publishing Company, 2005). Since then, through both my teaching and research, I have become committed to the human rights framework for policy development and its particular relevance to the issues and concerns related to an aging society. My research on employees with early symptoms of dementia highlighted the risks they face in the workplace while employed caregivers these impairments struggle to juggle caregiving and work responsibilities. Perhaps most provoking has been my empowerment work with grandparent caregivers who learned that they had rights for assistance and supports rather than just needs. Once empowered, they became strong community advocates for policy changes and services, underscoring for themselves and others their significant roles as creators of social capital.

The following chapters discuss many of the key issues and concerns confronting older adults in the United States and the policies formulated to deal with them. The ways in which these policies reflect human rights is key in each chapter. Chapter 1 presents the background on social policy and human rights and how they pertain to and impact older adults. Chapter 2 focuses on the Older Americans Act, the foundation of aging policy in the United States. Chapter 3 addresses economic supports for older adults, Chapter 4 examines policies associated with independence and autonomy, and Chapter 5 discusses physical and mental well-being. Chapter 6 focuses on employment and the workplace, Chapter 7 discusses policy and the family, Chapter 8 examines how policy relates to vulnerable populations of older adults, Chapter 9 discusses the ways in which various countries are developing policies for their older population and how these reflect human rights, while Chapter 10 discusses future policy challenges that must be met in order to ensure that rights of older adults are addressed.

Finally, I would like to acknowledge the assistance provided by Theresa Moran through her reviews and suggestions; for the enthusiastic support of Sheri W. Sussman, Executive Editor at Springer Publishing Company; and for the thoughtful comments and eternal patience of my husband, Colin.

Carole B. Cox

CHAPTER 1

Social Policy, Human Rights, and Older Adults

America is aging. Persons 65 years and older represent 12.9% of the population in the United States (Figure 1.1); by 2030, they will be 20% of the population (Administration on Aging, 2013). The population of the oldest old, those who are 85 and older, is rapidly increasing, as are the numbers of ethnic and minority populations. Older women continue to outnumber older men and approximately half of these women live alone. Social Security is the major source of income for 86% of older persons, and concerns about financial security and retirement plague many Americans. Although community and home supports for older adults needing assistance continue to expand, the majority of long-term care is provided by institutions. All of these issues are impacted by social policies that affect all Americans, as older adults are simply younger persons with additional years.

Social policy is enacted to address social problems and inequalities in society. It provides a course of action to be taken by a government (Rein, 1983) in response to these problems. Policy involves choices concerning benefits, allocations, and the sectors that are involved in the allocations (Gilbert & Terrell, 2012). It also includes decisions about the institutions that are responsible for addressing specific concerns and problems.

If policies are conceived as courses of actions to address problems in society, the first consideration must be how problems are identified and defined. This identification acts as the cornerstone for policy analysis

FIGURE 1.1 U.S. population 65 years and older: 1900–2050.

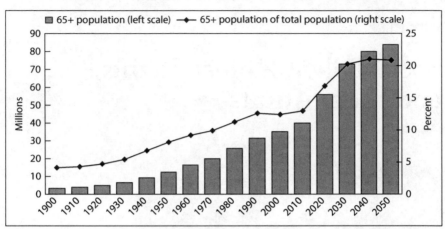

Source: 1900 to 1940, and 1960 to 1980, U.S. Bureau of the Census, 1983; 1950, U.S. Bureau of the Census, 1953; 1990, U.S. Bureau of the Census, 1992; 2000, U.S. Census Bureau, 2001; 2010, U.S. Census Bureau, 2011; 2020 to 2050, U.S. Census Bureau, 2012a; 1900 to 2010, decennial census; 2020 to 2050, 2012 *National Population Projections,* Middle series.

because it leads to the development of strategies and systems to solve the problem and produce positive, desired outcomes. All problems are not social problems. They become social problems when either they affect the quality of life of large groups of people or those in power express concern over those being affected (Chambers & Bonk, 2012). Consequently, it is critical to understand that the definition of issues such as homelessness or even access to health care as social problems depends to a large extent on the perspectives of those in power.

Policies that are developed to deal with social problems are not created in a vacuum. They are usually compromises between opposing views and perspectives. Thus, even if there is wide recognition and concern about long-term care, those in positions to enact policies frequently hold widely diverse perspectives on the best solutions and even on what the outcomes should be.

VALUES

Values are important influences on policy, with three of the most prominent being equality, equity, and adequacy. Equality refers to the same treatment for everyone, with benefits allocated equally to all persons who qualify. Equity is associated with fair treatment, in that people receive equity based on their contributions to society with some modifications made for the inability to contribute due to specific conditions that put them at a disadvantage. Adequacy connotes that benefit provides for a decent standard of living as it covers the costs of basic needs.

Two other concepts that influence policies are their institutional and residual perspectives (Wilensky & Lebeaux, 1965). Institutional perspective refers to policies as being part of the social system and views the provision of services and programs as the responsibility of society, with the focus on prevention and collective responsibility. In contrast, a residual policy is enacted only when other resources are insufficient and problems are beyond the ability of individuals to solve. The concepts reflect the extent to which needs or problems are perceived as due to the individual or society and who should be primarily responsible for meeting them.

Policy can also be distinguished on the basis of the principles of universality and selectivity. Universal policies are offered to all persons in society regardless of their means or needs, whereas selective policies are available only to those meeting specific criteria. Because they are available to all, universal policies do not have a stigma attached. Social Security is an example of a universal policy that is available to all who have contributed to the system. Conversely, selective policies focus on those who meet specific eligibility criteria and usually indicate that the recipient is unable to meet specific needs without assistance. Consequently, selective policies, such as Supplemental Security Income (SSI; Social Security), tend to have stigmas attached. Such stigmas can deter the use of programs.

In order for social policies to impact problems or conditions, they must have adequate resources. Without sufficient financing and commitment, it is impossible for them to reach selected goals. Consequently, without attention to the funding that they actually receive, they are at risk of being perceived as ineffective and even disbanded. Social policies must compete for scarce resources that are often in jeopardy as those in control of resources may doubt their significance or see them in conflict with other social or economic priorities or goals.

3

Moreover, during periods of sequestration when the federal government authorizes automatic spending cuts, the funding of social policies is particularly at risk.

SOCIAL POLICY AND AGING

Values play critical roles with respect to older persons, particularly when they need long-term care. Perhaps one of the primary areas of debate is whether long-term care is the responsibility of the individual, the family, or the government. Moreover, if it is a government concern, should it be under the purview of federal, state, or even local policy? Given these varying foci, it is little wonder that efforts to broaden and enhance long-term care to ensure that it adequately addresses the growing needs of an aging society have been slow to develop or keep pace with changing needs.

This dilemma is intensified by traditional values that underscore the autonomy of the family and its independence from government in conjunction with values that stress individual responsibility. As these values tend to be shared by both policy makers and their constituents, it is not surprising that older adults needing assistance and their families face the burdens often associated with such care on their own with little formal assistance or intervention. In fact, interventions are likely to be available and accessible only when the burden of care becomes overwhelming and informal resources are exhausted.

An inherent conflict exists between public support of dependent persons and the beliefs in self-reliance, autonomy, and protection from government intrusion. In a society that stresses productivity as a measure of self-worth, the actual value of those who are unproductive is sometimes questionable. At the same time, the belief in mutual support and the humanitarian ethic of providing for those less fortunate necessitates social responsibility for those unable to care for themselves.

Paternalism also pervades policies aimed at supporting older adults. This value is reflected in stereotypes and perceptions that view older persons with impairments as incapable of the same degree of self-fulfillment and self-realization as others in society. The result is that their options for self-determination can be severely limited as others are permitted to encroach upon their decision-making capacity and to act in their "best interest." As older persons with impairments are often unable to physically act on their decisions, they become vulnerable to coercion in long-term care (Collopy, 1988). To the extent that persons are treated in a discriminatory way on the basis of impairments rather than strengths, they are at further risk of dependency and the loss of their human rights.

Two concepts that are particularly relevant to responses toward older adults are those of "best interest" and the related concept of beneficence. *Best interest* is a term derived from the medical profession as it relates to the patient. However, it is frequently applied by agencies who decide on the services that they believe are in the older person's best interests. Unfortunately, this may not reflect the perception of the older person. For example, a person's ability to function independently may be threatened by others who question the person's ability to do so without assistance. Due to worries concerning the older person's welfare, family members and formal service providers may intervene and override the lifestyle or desires of the older adult. Though motivated by the best of intentions, such interventions threaten autonomy.

Policies are established to reach specific goals. With regard to older adults, specific goals are often blurred and may focus on prevention, maintenance, or restitution of functioning and independence. Moreover, these goals may compete with each other for resources, resulting in fragmented services and interventions. The result can be compromised policies that remain ineffective. Moreover, when goals are broad and undefined, it is difficult to determine the extent to which they are being reached and to evaluate the programs that they mandate. In fact, this vagueness makes assessing the appropriateness of the goals themselves difficult.

The family has traditionally been the main provider of care to older relatives needing assistance. Despite demographic changes, such as longer life spans, people having more extensive care needs, and fewer available caregivers, the family continues to play the major role in providing assistance (Feinberg, Reinhard, Houser, & Choula, 2011). At the same time, families themselves often require assistance and support as caregiving is frequently associated with burden and stress that can severely tax caregiver well-being and require particular interventions (Adelman, Tmanova, Delgado, Dion, & Lachs, 2014; Pearlin, Mullan, Semple, & Skaff, 1990; Pinquart & Sorensen, 2006). Thus, as older adults do not live in a vacuum, policies that address the concerns of their caregivers are also essential.

Evolving from traditions of the Elizabethan and Puritan societies, institutions have been the traditional places for care for dependent and impaired older persons without families or other informal supports. The poor houses and almshouses of the colonial era have become the nursing homes of American society and, for a long time, have provided the bulwark of care for those needing assistance. Consequently, community care has had to wrestle with this institutional bias. Although the majority of funds for long-term care continue to go to nursing homes, there has been a gradual increase in funding for community-based services (Reaves & Musumeci, 2014). Such services may promote the rights of older adults to remain independent and secure in the community.

HUMAN RIGHTS

Human rights provide the legal mandate to fulfill human needs (Wronka, 2008), and policy is the means by which these rights are enacted. Social policy includes choices among goals, outcomes, and even strategies that should improve the quality of life. As such, social policy based upon a human rights framework would provide every individual with guarantees for having needs met in a just society that recognizes such needs as fundamental to addressing human rights.

Human rights apply to everyone, regardless of where they live or who they are; it is a universal concept. Rights are also indivisible, meaning that governments and individuals must recognize each right and not selectively promote one over the other (Reichert, 2006). No one right is more important than another.

The concern about human rights and the need to protect vulnerable groups from abuses by those in power can be traced to the Code of Hammurabi (1750 BCE), which included 300 codes of ethical conduct dictating how persons should act toward one another. The ancient Greeks and Romans also wrote about civil and political rights while Judaism, Christianity, and Islam emphasized the inherent worth and dignity of each human being.

The focus on political rights was emphasized in the U.S. Declaration of Independence and Bill of Rights and in the French Declaration of the Rights of the Man and Citizen. Both of these documents outline political rights including rights to life, liberty, and the pursuit of happiness; freedom of speech, the press, and religion; and property rights, with the French Declaration addressing economic rights also (Wronka, 2008).

One of the worst horrors of World War II was the almost complete extermination of the Jews of Europe along with other groups such as the mentally ill and mentally challenged, gypsies, and homosexuals. The very right of these persons to exist was denied by those in power. Following the war, there was universal shock and a resolution that such a holocaust should not happen again. The war contributed to the establishment of the United Nations in 1945; in 1948, the General Assembly endorsed the Universal Declaration of Human Rights (UDHR; see the Appendix).

The document consists of 30 articles that have been subsequently elaborated upon by conventions, treaties, constitutions, and laws. The document establishes core principles that include universality of human rights, their interdependence and indivisibility, equality, and non-discrimination. Countries signing the Declaration are not legally bound to uphold it, although many of its principles are incorporated into their laws and policies.

The first set of rights (Articles 2–15) relates to political and individual freedoms, restricting the interference of governments, and is referred to as "negative rights." The second set of rights (Articles 16–27) focuses on an adequate standard of living including health and well-being, food, clothing, housing, medical care, and necessary social services that a country, according to its resources, must offer to all its residents. The third set of rights (Articles 28–30) promotes intergovernmental cooperation on global issues such as the environment and development, international peace, and international distributive justice. The UDHR has the status of law to which all countries must adhere.

Wronka (2008) groups these rights into five core notions that can assist in developing and understanding their application, as well as encourage the creation of a human rights culture: Human Dignity (Article 1); Non-Discrimination (Article 2); Civil and Political Rights (Articles 3–21), which enable persons to realize their human dignity through a country's laws and authority; Economic, Social, and Cultural Rights (Articles 22–27), which imply that governments must provide basic necessities to ensure that human dignity can be met; and Solidarity Rights (Articles 28–30), which deal with global issues such as pollution, war, development, and nationalism.

Subsequent to the UDHR, nine conventions or treaties have been passed that are intended to give full legal force to the declaration. When a government signs a convention, it is legally bound to uphold the standards that it sets. In the United States, the president may sign a convention or treaty; however, in order for it to become law, Congress must ratify it. To date, although the United States has signed seven of the nine major human rights treaties, which indicates its willingness and intent to abide by the purpose of each document, it has ratified only three: the International Covenant on Civil and Political Rights (1966), the International Convention of the Elimination of all forms of Racial Discrimination (1966), and the Convention Against Torture and Other Cruel, Inhuman, or Degrading Treatment of Punishment (1984).

The Covenant on Civil and Political Rights includes many articles that are directly pertinent to the lives and well-being of older persons. These include Article 1, the right to self-determination with the ability to pursue their economic, social, and cultural development; Article 16, everyone has the right to recognition before the law; and Article 26, all persons are equal before the law and entitled to equal protection.

The International Covenant of Economic, Social, and Cultural Rights that was passed in 1976 and which gives people a broad range of economic, social, and cultural rights—including the right to work, the right to the highest attainable standard of physical and mental health, and the right to take part in cultural life—has not been ratified by the United States, although the document was signed by President Carter in 1977. Fundamental to the Covenant is the right of self-determination and the mandate that those signing shall promote and respect the right. The Covenant also recognizes the right to have the highest attainable standard of physical and mental health, the right to an adequate standard of living, the right to work, and the right to partake in the cultural life of the society, including having access to scientific developments. Ratification followed by legislation and policies would have a major impact on inequality and the well-being of many groups in the country. However, once it is ratified, the United States would be subject to reporting and monitoring by an international committee.

Needs and Rights

Much attention in society is given to the needs of populations, particularly to the needs of specific groups. Consequently, needs are often confused with rights, or rights are obscured with the interest given to meeting specific needs. However, it is important to separate the two and to understand the differences, particularly as policies often work toward meeting needs without any mention of rights.

Ife (2006) discusses how needs exist as phenomena that can be objectively identified and measured. Thus, needs for food, housing, and supports are measured through tools such as "needs assessments." However, needs are also associated with values that in themselves determine whether "needs" exist and even how they should be met. Consequently, the assessor and his or her perspective and values are influential in determining whether an older adult requires support or new housing, as well as what types of support to provide.

In addition, needs are generally not ends in themselves. Persons have needs in order for something else to occur. Thus, an older person has a need for a home attendant in order to remain independent or a need for home-delivered meals in order to remain healthy. Such needs are related to underlying human rights: the right to life, liberty, and security of person.

Maslow, who articulated the role of human needs (1943) in development, provides a framework for a hierarchy of needs beginning with physiological needs and leading to safety, needs for belongingness and love, and the ultimate need or goal of self-actualization. This highest need can only be met when more basic human needs have been realized.

In contrast, human rights are seen as equally important factors in our humanity that cannot be ranked; they are indivisible.

An important point regarding needs and rights is that when persons perceive that their need is actually a human right, they are then more likely to make demands that it is met. People are empowered when they understand that what they had considered a need is actually a right that society is obliged to fulfill. Knowing one's rights makes persons less vulnerable to the abuses of others while also presenting a platform for advocacy and change.

Older People and Human Rights

As people age, they are vulnerable to increasing dependency, frailty, and discrimination by societies. The change in their status from that of independent to dependent, from valuable to less valuable, means that their rights are often violated. Moreover, their very dignity, a right underscored in the preamble of the Universal Declaration on Human Rights, is often ignored or threatened. With rights perceived as indivisible, discrimination based on age erodes human dignity and diminishes the status of older adults with regards to others in society. This discrimination is reflected in a lack of opportunity, inadequate income support and health care, and fewer resources with fewer options for living a secure life with their rights fulfilled.

Older people are not specifically recognized as a group under the Universal Declaration of Rights, nor have they been in conventions subsequent to the Declaration. Thus, although there have been conventions and declarations on the rights of other specific groups—such as the Convention on the Elimination of All Forms of Discrimination Against Women (CEDAW), Convention on the Elimination of All Forms of Racial Discrimination (CERD), Convention on the Rights of the Child, and Convention on the Rights of Persons With Disabilities— there has been no UN convention on the rights of older persons. The rights of older adults are implicitly but not explicitly referred to in the Covenants on Economic, Social and Cultural Rights and on Civil and

Political Rights; CEDAW; and the Convention on the Rights of Persons with Disabilities.

The concerns related to older persons have received much attention. In 1991, the UN issued a document, Principles for Older Persons (United Nations, 1991), emphasizing that priority should be given to the situation of older persons, particularly in the following five areas:

- Independence—Older persons should have access to adequate food, water, shelter, clothing, and health care through the provision of income, family, and community support and self-help. Older persons should have the opportunity to work and to participate in determining when to retire. Older persons should be able to reside at home for as long as possible.

- Participation—Older persons should remain integrated in society, participate actively in the formulation and implementation of policies that directly affect their well-being, and share their knowledge and skills with younger generations. Older persons should be able to serve as volunteers in positions appropriate to their interests and capabilities and to form associations.

- Care—Older persons should benefit from family and community care and have access to adequate and appropriate health care. Older persons should have access to social and legal services to enhance their autonomy, protection, and care.

- Self-fulfillment—Older persons should be able to pursue opportunities for the full development of their potential. Older persons should have access to the educational, cultural, spiritual, and recreational resources of society.

- Dignity—Older persons should be able to live in dignity and security and be free of exploitation and physical or mental abuse.

Since that time, there have been a series of reports on the status of older people, regional meetings, and the establishment of a standing committee on the rights of older persons at the UN. However, there has not been a UN convention on the rights of older people, which is perceived as necessary to ensure that rights are actually realized (HelpAge International, 2010).

The Madrid International Plan of Action on Ageing (MIPAA; United Nations, 2002) presents a plan for the rights of older persons; however, in contrast to rights that are codified in conventions or treaties, it is not legally binding to any government. Although the MIPAA has been endorsed by the General Assembly of the UN, policies to carry it out remain scarce and inconsistent. Consequently, governments have only a moral responsibility to adhere to recommendations rather than a legal commitment, and monitors of human rights violations and commitments seldom include the rights of older persons in their reports (HelpAge International, 2010).

A report to the UN Secretary General in 2011 focuses specifically on the challenges to human rights that an older population presents (OHCHR, 2011). Although older persons are not a homogenous group, the following challenges exist in both developed and developing countries:

- Discrimination on the basis of age
- Poverty with homelessness, malnutrition, unattended chronic disease, unaffordable medicines and treatments, and income insecurity, which includes the fact that older persons are often the primary caregivers for grandchildren and other family members
- Violence and abuse—including physical, emotional, and/or sexual abuse and financial exploitation
- Lack of specific measures and services, particularly specialized services such as residential and long-term home care and geriatric services

As summarized in the report, government efforts to protect the rights of older persons have been "inconsistent, scattered, and insufficient with a general lack of comprehensive, target legal and institutional frameworks." Among the areas requiring more attention and work are:

- Violence against older persons and women in particular
- Financial exploitation
- Health

- Long-term care
- Participation in policy making and political life
- Work

SOCIAL POLICY AND RIGHTS

As social policies aim to address the needs of citizens, they should integrate standards that move beyond meeting basic needs to assure that fundamental rights are being met. For example, people do not simply need adequate medical care; they have a fundamental right to it. The responsibility for meeting these rights rests with the government that develops policies and programs to enact them.

The Office of the High Commissioner on Human Rights/United Nations Development Project (OHCHR/UNDP) developed a tool for assessing human rights in policies (2004). The first step in the process is to identify the problem and the human rights that are affected. Step 2 is setting priorities and determining for whom it is most important and why it is a priority. Step 3 identifies the actors involved, those who are affected by the problem, and those who can affect it. This step involves understanding the power blocks, economic interests, political interests, and other social groups that may be related to the problem and to the claim holders and duty bearers. Gathering information is the next step; such information may be reviewed according to human rights checklists and indicators. The next step is the analysis, which focuses on the underlying cause of the problems, the rights that are involved, and who is affected and why. A capacity analysis is also done, which examines what is causing the vulnerability of certain groups and determines the capacity of the duty bearers to respect and fulfill their human rights obligations. The analysis concludes with what next steps are required to assure that rights are recognized.

Indicators help to measure the progress being made toward specific human rights benchmarks or targets, such as the proportion of older persons receiving transportation assistance or preventive health care examinations. However, the first step toward benchmarks is agreement on what the indicators actually are (www.ohchr.org). Indicators may be either quantitative or qualitative (OHCHR, 2012). Quantitative indicators could be the number of older persons in institutions, the proportion who receive assistance from family, or the ratio of persons over 65 below the poverty level. Qualitative refers to the comments or information that persons provide, such as opinions or perceptions of how well rights are being met, that complement the objective indicators. Countries need to develop their own indicators so that they are relevant to their context. Consequently, the prevalence of malnutrition among the elderly may be an appropriate indicator in developing countries while that of supportive housing may be more appropriate for developed countries.

A rights-based framework for understanding policy focuses on how rights are emphasized rather than on how human needs are met. Boesen and Martin (2007) present a guide for analyzing social policies that recognizes individual and group rights as claims that persons are empowered to make and to which they are entitled. The approach focuses on the structure and the barriers within the state that prevent rights from being realized.

According to the framework, programs should focus on the most vulnerable groups in a society, giving attention to the structural conditions that are responsible for their vulnerability. Programs should then be comprehensive about meeting rights and expanding choices and abilities to exercise rights of discussion, association, and freedom. Rights-based programs focus on the relationship between rights holders and duty bearers, those responsible for fulfilling the rights. Thus, duty bearers need to be held accountable to policies and laws and their obligations. Rights holders need to be supported in networks that enable them to become more engaged in the government and in claiming their rights. The focus is on the core problems that the policy is addressing, the rights issues involved, and the target groups (the duty bearers). Formulating clear standards and objectives, with the participation of the rights holders in designing the policies, is a core part of the process. Rights holders become empowered through awareness and capacity building, while duty bearers learn to be accountable and responsive to them.

SUMMARY

Developing social policy is a complicated process that occurs through distinct stages and encompasses many components, ranging from problem identification to values to goals. Once established, the effectiveness of policies depends on the extent to which they are perceived as priorities and the resources allocated to them. Many policies fall short in incorporating human rights principles. Policies tend to focus on needs, which are often identified and prioritized by those in power with little or no attention given to the views and perspectives of those who would be affected. The very policies that disenfranchise older adults serve as barriers to the realization of their human rights.

Policies that focus on older adults often emphasize traditional values, such as beneficence and paternalism, that can actually undermine their status and human rights. Moreover, as policies tend to work toward meeting specific needs, they do not necessarily address human rights. As age continues to form a basis for discrimination, the rights of older adults remain in jeopardy. Moreover, as age itself can present a barrier to full participation in society, older adults are vulnerable to exclusion, which compounds their vulnerability to having their rights ignored.

A convention on the rights of older people has been proposed as essential to guaranteeing their rights. Such a convention would substantiate, promote, and protect older people's rights, with those signing the convention obligated to meet them. Among its other outcomes would be clarifying the responsibilities of duty bearers and rights holders, giving greater focus to the economic and social rights of older adults with more attention to age discrimination, acting as an advocacy and education tool for older people, and shifting the paradigm from older people as recipients of welfare to their position as rights holders (Global Alliance for the Rights of Older People, 2014).

The population of the United States, compared to that of other developed and developing countries, is aging. Policies that reflect this demographic change are critical for both individual and social well-being. Policies that continue to exclude or differentiate older adults from the rest of society infringe on their human rights while also inhibiting their ability to continue as participating and productive members of society. Assuring that policies comply with human rights principles is the cornerstone of a just society.

QUESTIONS FOR DISCUSSION

1. Discuss some of the factors associated with the effectiveness of a social policy.
2. How do values affect social policy for older adults? Give specific examples.
3. In what ways do needs differ from rights? Why is it important to distinguish between them?
4. What are some of the reasons given for having a UN convention on the rights of older people?

REFERENCES

Adelman, R., Tmanova, L., Delgado, D., Dion, S., & Lachs, M. (2014). Caregiver burden: A clinical review. *JAMA, 311*, 1052–1060.

Administration on Aging. (2013). *A profile of older Americans*. Washington, DC: Administration for Community Living, U.S. Department of Health and Human Services.

Boesen, J., & Martin, T. (2007). *Applying a rights-based approach: An inspirational guide for civil society*. Retrieved from http://www.acfid.asn.au/aid-issues/files/applying-a-rights-based-approach-2013-an-inspirational-guide-for-civil-society

Chambers, D., & Bonk, J. (2012). *Social policy and social programs: A method for the practical public policy analyst* (6th ed.). New York, NY: Pearson.

Collopy, B. (1988). Autonomy in long term care, some crucial distinctions. *The Gerontologist, 28*, 10–18.

Feinberg, L., Reinhard, S., Houser, A., & Choula, R. (2011). *Valuing the invaluable: 2011 update on the contributions and costs of family caregiving*. Washington, DC: AARP Public Policy Institute.

Gilbert, N., & Terrell, P. (2012). *Dimensions of social welfare policy* (8th ed.). New York, NY: Pearson.

Global Alliance for the Rights of Older People. (2014). *Why we need a convention*. Retrieved from http://www.rightsofolderpeople.org/why-we-need-a-convention/

HelpAge International. (2010). *Strengthening older people's rights: Towards a UN convention*. Retrieved from http://www.helpage.org/what-we-do/rights/strengthening-older-peoples-rights-towards-a-convention/

Ife, J. (2006). *Human rights and social work: Towards rights based practice.* New York, NY: Cambridge University Press.

Maslow, A. (1943). A theory of human motivation. *Psychological Review, 50,* 370–396.

Office of the High Commissioner of Human Rights. (2011). *Summary of the report of the Secretary General to the General Assembly*. Retrieved from http://www.ohchr.org/EN/Issues/OlderPersons/Pages/OlderPersonsIndex.aspx

Office of the High Commissioner of Human Rights. (2012). *Human rights indicators: A guide to measurement and implementation*. Retrieved from http://www.ohchr.org/Documents/Issues/HRIndicators/Summary_en.pdf

Office of the High Commissioner of Human Rights/UN Development Project. (2004). *Methodology and tools for human rights-based assessment and analysis.* Geneva, Switzerland: OHCHR and UNDP.

Pearlin, L., Mullan, J., Semple, S., & Skaff, M. (1990). Caregiving and the stress process: An overview of concepts and their measures. *The Gerontologist, 30,* 583–594.

Pinquart, M., & Sorensen, S. (2006). Gender differences in caregiver stressors, social resources and health: An updated meta-analysis. *Journal of Gerontology: Social Sciences, 61,* P33–P45.

Reaves, E., & Musumeci. (2014). *Medicaid and long-term services and supports: A primer*. Kaiser Commission on Medicaid. Retrieved from http://kff.org/medicaid/report/medicaid-and-long-term-services-and-supports-a-primer/

Reichert, E. (2006). *Understanding human rights: An exercise book.* Thousand Oaks, CA: Sage.

Rein, M. (1983). *From policy to practice.* Armonk, NY: M.E. Sharpe.

United Nations. (1991). *Principles for older persons.* Retrieved from http://www.un-documents.net/pop.htm

United Nations. (2002). *Political Declaration and Madrid International Plan of Action on Ageing.* New York, NY: Second World Assembly on Ageing, United Nations.

U.S. Bureau of the Census. (2012). *National Population Projections (middle series).*

Wilensky, H., & Lebeaux, C. (1965). *Industrial society and social welfare. The impact of industrialization on the supply and organization of social welfare services in the United States.* New York, NY: Free Press.

Wronka, J. (2008). *Human rights and social justice.* Thousand Oaks, CA: Sage.

CHAPTER 2

The Framework for Federal Involvement: The White House Conference on Aging and the Older Americans Act

The government's involvement with older adults is directly expressed through policies that mandate and offer support to programs and services that can help to ensure their well-being and community participation. The Older Americans Act (OAA) passed in 1965 provides a foundation for such involvement through its original mandate to serve all older Americans through a plethora of services and supports designed to help maintain the independence, security, and well-being of older adults.

WHITE HOUSE CONFERENCES ON AGING

In 1958, legislation was introduced that asked for a White House Conference on Aging, which would bring together persons from all parts of the country to make policy recommendations that would focus on the economic security of older persons. Consequently, the first White House Conference on Aging was held in 1961, with more than 3,000 participants and representatives of nearly 300 organizations. The conference led to the passage of the 1961 Social Security amendments,

Medicare and Medicaid, and the OAA. It also called for a conference to be held every 10 years; this conference would focus on setting policies for the aging for the following decade.

The 1971 conference was attended by more than 4,000 persons. Prior to the conference, 6,000 community forums had been held throughout the country in which persons discussed their issues and problems. When presented in the conference, 163 of these policy proposals were adopted (U.S. Senate Special Committee on Aging, 1971).

Human rights were a cornerstone of the conference, which was organized around education, employment and retirement, physical and mental health, housing and environment, income, nutrition, retirement roles and activities, spiritual well-being, and transportation. These were considered as basic rights that were pertinent to all older persons. The other subjects—facilities, programs and services, government and non-government organizations, planning and demonstration, and training for services in the field of aging—were classified as the mechanisms for meeting these needs, which were the responsibilities of those in power (duty bearers).

The conference concluded with recommendations of detailed plans and services that were essential for meeting these rights. Among the recommendations that were subsequently implemented were the nutrition program for the elderly, which helped to establish a national hot meals program; increased funding for the OAA; and the establishment of the Senate Special Committee on Aging and the Federal Council on Aging.

The 1981 conference was the first to use a quota system for delegates to ensure adequate representation by specific subgroups: women, minorities, and the disabled. Prior to the conference, these subgroups were encouraged to hold their own caucuses to frame issues for the conference. The conference resulted in recommendations for policies that would improve the economic well-being of older persons, expand housing, increase availability and quality of health care, increase comprehensiveness of social service delivery systems, promote more employment opportunities, develop a comprehensive long-term care policy, develop a national retirement policy, and overcome false stereotypes about aging. In addition, it recognized the role older persons can play as a national resource. It also recommended that the federal government's role with regards to volunteer programs, such as the Foster Grandparent Program, the Retired Senior Volunteer Program (RSVP), the Senior Companion Program, and the Senior Community Service Employment program, be expanded.

Again, reflective of the influence of human rights, the conference gave attention to the barriers that prevented full community participation by older adults, including age discrimination, negative attitudes and stereotypes, a lack of transportation and access to programs, security concerns, and a lack of information. As a result, the conference created a list of recommendations to the government that would help to overcome these barriers and thereby increase full participation of older persons. However, the development of these proposals was complicated by the disparity among the stakeholders themselves, with strong divisions between national and regional perspectives (Hanham, 1983). Such divisions continue to impact policy development as the roles of federal and local governments are often in dispute.

More than 125,000 people participated in planning and in mini conferences in preparation for the 1995 White House Conference. These preconference events led to 60 resolutions that were sent to the conference for consideration, where 80 additional resolutions were presented. The resolutions were grouped into four thematic categories: (1) Assuring Comprehensive Health Care, including Long-Term Care; (2) Promoting Economic Security; (3) Maximizing Housing and Support Service Options; and (4) Maximizing Options for a Quality Life. The majority, 41, of the 60 resolutions were passed, with all reflecting human rights.

Following the conference, the policy committee reworked the resolutions to eliminate overlap and developed implementation strategies. Among the key outcomes were the importance given to the parity between health and mental health services, the need for increasing the minimum wage, and raising the outside earnings limit under Social Security. For the first time, national attention was given to kinship care and the specific role that grandparents play in raising grandchildren. The delegates also concurred on their opposition to proposed cuts in Medicare as well as establishing pension equity for women.

The last White House Conference, held in 2005, had the theme "The Booming Dynamics of Aging: From Awareness to Action." Delegates were asked to create a blueprint for aging for the next 10 years. The conference was attended by 1,200 delegates who voted on 73 resolutions that were formed in the preconference meetings. The two most-supported resolutions were the reauthorization of the OAA and the need for a coordinated and comprehensive long-term care strategy. One of the top resolutions was the creation of a national strategy for promoting elder justice through prevention and prosecution of elder abuse (WHCOA, 2005). Strengthening Medicare and Medicaid, expanding geriatric training, developing new models of long-term care, and improving mental health care for older people were among the resolutions that were passed for implementation. For the first time, a resolution calling for accountability and oversight of the implementation of the resolutions was also passed.

Two significant issues plagued the conference. This was the first meeting that a president did not attend, and attendees, in contrast to earlier meetings, were not permitted to introduce or modify any of the policy resolutions. Particularly troubling to many was that no alternatives could be given to the Bush administration-backed resolutions supporting the privatizing of Medicare and Social Security (Stoil, 2006).

The next White House Conference is scheduled to be held in 2015. Although the Administration for Community Living (U.S. Department of Health and Human Services [DHHS], 2014) has requested conference funding of $3,000,000, it has not yet been allocated.

White House Conferences and Human Rights

The White House Conferences on Aging reflect many human rights principles. Older persons actively participate in the planning of the conferences and also in the decisions and resolutions that are passed. Since the first conference, these resolutions have underscored many of the pertinent issues regarding human rights affecting older adults, with an emphasis on them as rights rather than needs. The resolutions also detail the obligations of government to address these issues.

Following the human rights agenda, the indicators for these issues are based on both quantitative and qualitative data collected through caucuses held before the conference. Although many resolutions have resulted in policies, their effectiveness in reaching stated goals is often compromised by a lack of commitment by the duty bearers in power.

THE OLDER AMERICANS ACT

An outcome of the 1961 White House Conference on Aging was the passage of the Older Americans Act (PL-89-73) in 1965. The Act remains the federal government's only comprehensive policy toward improving the lives of its older population. The original objectives of the Act included improving persons' lives with respect to income, housing, employment, retirement, and community services, and assuring that older adults had freedom, independence, and the exercise of their own initiative in planning and managing their lives (National Association of State Units on Aging, 1982). At the signing of the OAA, President Lyndon Johnson exclaimed:

> No longer will older Americans be denied the healing miracle of modern medicine. No longer will illness crush and destroy the savings that they have so carefully put away over a lifetime so that they might enjoy dignity in their later years. No longer will young families see their own incomes, and their own hopes, eaten away simply because they are carrying out their deep moral obligations to their parents, and to their uncles, and to their aunts. And no longer will this nation refuse the hand of justice to those who have given a lifetime of service and wisdom and labor to the progress of this progressive country.
>
> www.dhs.state.or.us/spd/tools/cm/oaa/
> history_mar06.pdf

The Act established the Administration on Aging (AOA) to administer the programs and to serve as a focal point for information on aging. The AOA serves as the federal focal point for the Act and for its policy and services. These are carried out through 56 State Units on

Aging (SUA) and 629 Area Agencies on Aging (AAA). In 2012, the AOA became part of the Administration for Community Living (ACL), the administrator of which is also the Assistant Secretary for Aging.

The SUAs and AAAs, which comprise the network for providing services under the Act, receive funding that is primarily based on the percentage of the state's and area's population that is 60 years and older. Federal funds are required to be matched at rates of 15% or 25% of their allocations. The funds are used for planning, developing, and coordinating these services. Under the Act, each AAA must have an advisory council that is involved in developing and coordinating the local plan and its services. Reflecting the right of community participation, more than 50% of the members of the council must be older adults who represent the interests of those in the community.

In the fiscal year 2012, approximately $1.4 billion and $22 million, respectively, were provided for services under Titles III (Community Services) and VII (Vulnerable Elders) of the OAA (U.S. Government Accounting Office [GAO], 2012). Nearly 11 million older Americans and their caregivers received services, with the majority living below the poverty threshold (GAO, 2012).

Amendments to the OAA

The original objectives of the Act listed in the following parallel many human rights issues found in the Universal Declaration of Human Rights (UNDHR):

1. An adequate income in retirement in accordance with the American standard of living.
2. The best possible physical and mental health which science can make available and without regard to economic status.
3. Obtaining and maintaining suitable housing, independently selected, designed and located with reference to special needs and available at costs which older citizens can afford.
4. Full restorative services for those who require institutional care, and a comprehensive array of community-based, long-term care services adequate to appropriately sustain older people in their

communities and in their homes, including support to family members and other persons providing voluntary care to older individuals needing long-term care services.

5. Opportunity for employment with no discriminatory personnel practices because of age.

6. Retirement in health, honor, dignity—after years of contribution to the economy.

7. Participating in and contributing to meaningful activity within the widest range of civic, cultural, educational and training and recreational opportunities.

8. Efficient community services, including access to low cost transportation, which provide a choice in supported living arrangements and social assistance in a coordinated manner and which are readily available when needed, with emphasis on maintaining a continuum of care for vulnerable older individuals.

9. Immediate benefit from proven research knowledge which can sustain and improve health and happiness.

10. Freedom, independence, and the free exercise of individual initiative in planning and managing their own lives, full participation in the planning and operation of community based services and programs provided for their benefit, and protection against abuse, neglect, and exploitation.

The Act was amended in 2006 (PL 109-365) and consists of the following seven titles:

Title I—Declaration of Objectives

Title II—Establishment of the Administration on Aging as the office in the federal government responsible for developing and offering services, and the roles of the Assistant Secretary of Aging.

Title III—Grants for State and Community Programs in Aging, including the establishment of state agencies on aging and area agencies on aging. The role of these agencies is to act as advocates on behalf of and to coordinate social service programs for older people.

Title IV—Activities for Health, Independence, and Longevity

Title V—Community Service Senior Opportunities Act

Title VI—Grants for Native Americans

Title VII—Allotments for Vulnerable Elder Rights Activities

Since the 1970s, the amendments to the Act have targeted services for the most vulnerable older adults, those with the greatest social and economic needs. These are persons over 60 who have incomes at or below the poverty threshold, have physical or mental impairments, or are culturally, socially, or geographically isolated.

The 1975 amendments mandated state and local agencies to develop programs in the areas of transportation and home services in order to assist the impaired elderly. System optimizing was to be accomplished through special funding allocated to ombudsman projects, services to meet the needs of those not being adequately served, and ambulatory day care services. These areas were consolidated in 1978 into three categories: access services (transportation, outreach, information, and referral); in-home services (home health aide, homemaker, telephone reassurance, chore maintenance); and legal services.

The 1987 amendments authorized funds specifically for nonmedical in-home services for the frail elderly. This group includes those having a physical or mental disability, Alzheimer's disease, or a related disorder with neurological or organic brain dysfunction that restricts the ability to perform daily tasks or to function independently. Amendments also required that state plans identify and coordinate planning, and assess the needs for services for older disabled individuals.

The 1992 amendments placed greater focus on caregivers and added a new title, Title VII, Vulnerable Elder Rights Activities. Title VII recognized that many older adults were suffering in the community, denied their basic rights and benefits, and required vigorous advocacy. The amendment brought together the long-term care ombudsman program, elder rights and legal assistance, benefits outreach and counseling, and programs for the prevention of elder abuse and neglect.

The amendments of 2000 retained the focus on low-income minorities but also included those living in rural areas. The emphasis on access services, in-home services, and legal assistance continues with efforts focused on more flexibility to states and AAAs in developing their systems.

Particularly relevant to the support of the older adult in the community was the enactment of The National Family Caregiver Support Program (NFCSP). The program provides funds to states to develop five basic services for family caregivers: information about services; assistance in gaining access to supportive services; individual counseling, support groups, and caregiver training; respite care; and supplemental services to complement the care given by caregivers. States may also allocate up to 10% of the caregiver funds to grandparents raising grandchildren. Priority is given to persons with the greatest social and economic need and to older adults caring for persons with mental retardation and developmental disabilities.

Congress reauthorized the Act in 2006, providing funding through 2011. Amendments to the Act included targeting older adults at risk of institutional placement and those with limited English proficiency. The phrase "Choices for Independence" was also added. This requires states and the AAAs to promote home and community-based long-term care in order to prevent or delay institutionalization and to empower consumers so that they can make informed decisions about their options, a change that firmly sustains the Act's focus on human rights.

The AAAs were also encouraged to provide information on their area plans on livable communities. The AOA was also given the responsibilities of developing and implementing systems for elder justice, conducting an elder abuse incidence study, and providing grants to states to undertake new elder justice activities including financial literacy and elder shelters. In addition, the AOA was given the authority to develop Aging and Disability Resource Centers (ADRCs) in all states. These ADRCs are intended to be access points for long-term care services that can keep people in their homes. Title IV asked for new model projects on aging in place, improving transportation and mental health screening and treatment. Title V emphasized including training in the community employment. There was a greater focus on the mental health of older persons, although there were no specific amendments or requirements related to it.

In the fiscal year 2012, the OAA received a total of $1.9 billion with 71% of the funds going to Title III, Grants for State and Community Programs in Aging, which is reflective of the major role played by these supportive services. Title III contains all of the services needed to help older adults remain independent in the community, including access services, in-home services, and community services.

Title III-B Home and Community-Based Supportive Services

Access Services

Having accurate information is essential to independence as it is basic to connecting those in need with services and providers. Consequently, an entry point into the service system that offers access to the array of available programs was created with the eldercare locator.

The eldercare locator is available both through the Internet and by telephone. Its goal is to assist persons to access services by providing them with immediate information services and resources. It also links people with resources in their community. The locator links persons to a website (benefitscheckup.org/) that assists them to find benefits as well as to determine their eligibility.

Two other websites funded by the AAA are the National Clearinghouse for Long-Term Care Information, which provides detailed information on planning for long-term care needs, and the National Alzheimer's Call Center, which provides advice, information, and consultation on Alzheimer's disease.

Access also includes transportation services, which can further enable many vulnerable older adults to remain in the community. The role of transportation in meeting the needs of this population is indicated in a 2010 study of transportation conducted by AOA (AOA Research Brief, 2012b). In 2010, AOA-funded services provided for 25.6 million rides, and the riders, in comparison to the general population, were more likely to be older, female, living alone, residing in a nonmetropolitan area, in poor health, and requiring functional assistance.

Other data used to indicate the outcome of Title III access services reveal that case management services provided more than 3.6 million hours of assistance with managers assessing needs, developing care plans, and arranging services in 2012 (DHHS, 2012). Eighty percent of the users of the service reported that, as a result of case management, they were better able to care for themselves. Research also suggests that case management serves a population at risk of institutionalization and that participants believe that the services they receive are sufficient in linking them with other programs that assist them to remain in the community (Leary, 2007).

However, questions remain about the extent to which home and community services meet the needs of minority seniors and their caregivers (Herrera, George, Angel, Markides, & Torres-Gil, 2013). Their study of service use in 2009 showed that Hispanics had the highest rate of unmet hours of care and that caregiver services were less likely to help African Americans remaining at home than other groups. Despite their greater levels of disability, services were underused by minority populations. These important findings suggest that more outreach to these populations is necessary if their needs and rights are to be met.

IN-HOME SERVICES

Personal care services are particularly important in helping older adults to remain in the community (Chen & Thompson, 2010). According to AOA data (DHHS, 2012), more than 27 million hours of personal care was provided in 2010. These data on the characteristics of those served show that over 70% of those receiving services were over 75 years, in poor health and living alone. A large section needed assistance with more than three activities of daily living (ADLs). Although service users reported high satisfaction with the service, they also appear dissatisfied with the number of hours they received each week, with 44% stating they wanted more homemaker hours. Other factors related to dissatisfaction were being a minority, living in a rural/suburban area, and having high ADL impairment.

Family Caregiver Support Program

The Family Caregiver Support Program, Title III-E of the OAA, focuses on providing services for family caregivers. In 2010, nearly 11 million older persons and their caregivers received assistance through the program (AOA, 2013). Funds are given to states with a required match for services including information and referral; service coordination/case management; counseling, support groups, and training; respite care; and supplemental services that can help them with their caregiving.

A 2009 study of participants found that 47% were adult children caring for a parent and 39% were spousal caregivers. Spousal caregivers were more likely to be older than 70 years, and to have poor health themselves. The majority of spouses caring for someone 85 years or older were themselves over 80 years. Participants reported that the most useful service was respite care. The majority, 80%, rated the services as excellent and felt that they enabled them to provide care for a longer period (Foster & Kleinman, 2011).

A multistate review of the program found that states that had previously recognized and provided services for caregivers were better able to implement the programs and provide support and training for caregivers (Giunta, 2010). The findings also revealed barriers to the effectiveness of the programs, which included limited financial support, lack of public awareness of the program, and lack of uniform assessment tools to determine needs.

COMMUNITY SERVICES

Legal Assistance

Funding is provided by OAA to those states that give it to the local AAAs for legal services. In 2010, this resulted in more than 1,000 separate agreements with legal service providers who delivered nearly 1 million hours of assistance (McMillion, 2011). However, it is estimated that the need for assistance is four times greater than that which is available. In 2010, legal assistance to low-income elderly met less than 25% of the need for those living at or below the poverty line (Godfrey, 2010). Consequently, many were without the assistance they needed to assure their legal and their human right to a fair and public hearing.

In order to meet the needs of older persons in a better manner, particularly those with the greatest needs, and to help ensure their rights, the American Bar Association (ABA) outlined priorities that needed to be addressed in the reauthorization of the OAA: target scarce resources to those least able to advocate on their own behalf; develop and maintain high-quality assistance systems at the state level that give priority to the needs of target groups and that coordinate resources for maximum impact; strengthen the entities responsible for developing and coordinating each state's legal services and rights programs for older people; and provide adequate funding. In order to use resources more efficiently, restructuring of the system has been suggested by changing the contract systems that the AAAs use for providers to a single statewide legal service provider that will have greater accountability (Godfrey, 2012).

Adult Day Care

Data from 2012 show that there were 4,800 adult day centers serving 273,200 participants in the country (Centers for Disease Control and Prevention [CDC], 2012). Centers provide a setting for persons with chronic diseases who require supervised care. They are also becoming providers of transitional care and short-term rehabilitation following hospitalization. Nearly half of all participants have some level of dementia. Findings from a study by MetLife (2010) show that there is an average of one direct care worker for every six participants and nearly 80% of centers have a nursing professional on staff. The centers are also a major source of respite for family caregivers, with over 80% of participants attending full days and 46% attending five days a week. However, adequate funding is a major challenge for the centers as they deal with more complicated care needs, adequate staffing, and physical space (Anderson, Dabelko-Schoeny, & Tarrant, 2012).

Senior Centers

Senior centers act as community focal points under the OAA as they connect persons to other services. There are nearly 11,000 senior centers serving one million persons every day (NISC, 2010). The majority of participants are women and more than half live alone, with Caucasians, African Americans, Hispanics, and Asians comprising most of the population. Compared to others their age, those attending senior centers have better health, more social interaction and life satisfaction, and lower incomes than their nonattending peers. Most attend the center 1 to 3 times per week, averaging 3.3 hours per visit (NISC, 2010). Centers appear to play important roles in the lives of participants as they are sources of friendships, learning, and belonging (Gitelson et al., 2008).

Funding comes from many sources beyond the AAA and includes federal, state, and local grants, as well as private foundations. Among the challenges faced by centers are maintaining sufficient funding for services, attracting and keeping volunteers, maintaining adequate space, providing transportation for participants, and offering relevant and innovative programs (Dichele, 2013).

Nutrition Services

Nutrition services are the oldest of the OAA programs. The objective of the nutrition program is to reduce hunger and food insecurity and to promote socialization, health, and well-being of older people by helping them to gain access to nutritional and other health promotion services that prevent the onset of poor health conditions. In addition to providing meals, they provide nutrition counseling and education. The congregate sites also provide socialization as well as a means for older participants to act as volunteers. Meals are offered throughout the community in senior centers, churches, and community centers.

In addition, to congregate meal programs, the OAA program also provides home-delivered meals to older homebound persons. This program also acts as an access point to other community services. In the fiscal year 2010, about 60% of the total meals provided through the nutrition program were home-delivered, in comparison to 40% served at congregate sites (AOA, 2013). The total appropriation for both congregate and home-delivered meals in 2012 was $439,070,000; this is the same amount that was allocated in 2011, and a decrease in funding from the fiscal year 2010.

Consequently, we need to know whether the program is truly meeting the population's needs. As an example, a study of the nutrition program in Georgia (Lee, Sinnett, Bengl, Johnson, & Brown, 2011) found that about 60% of persons requesting services in 2008 were placed on waitlists. These people, particularly those requesting home-delivered meals, represented the most vulnerable, with poorer health status, food insecurity, and nutritional risk. Equally disturbing is that those who classified themselves as "other race/not disclosing race" and living alone were more likely to be put on the waitlist.

OAA AND HUMAN RIGHTS

The OAA clearly reflects the rights of older adults through a myriad of services that offer support, security, and protection to all older adults in the community. The support of the family is a critical aspect of its programs. Concomitantly, in its focus on the most vulnerable, it is involved in meeting critical needs that seriously undermine the independence of many elderly.

Studies show that persons using Title III programs tend to use multiple services, transportation and home-delivered meals, and congregate meals. These persons were most likely to be in poverty, living alone, unmarried, and have difficulty with multiple ADLs (Barrett & Schimmel, 2010). A survey that compared persons receiving Title III services in 2009 to older Americans not receiving such services found that participants older than their peers were more likely to be in poverty and living alone (Altshuler & Schimmel, 2010). They were at higher risk of nursing home placement, with those receiving homemaker services, home-delivered meals, and case management particularly vulnerable in terms of remaining in the community.

The most complete evaluation of Title III programs is available with the Government Accounting Office (GAO, 2011), which examined national data on older Americans and Title III programs. It found that in 2008 about 5% of persons over 60 years received home-based care or meals under Title III, but that most low-income adults in need of these services did not receive them. According to program directors, the need for the meals was greater than the funding permitted. In addition, between the years 1990 and 2008, there was an increase in the number of persons requesting home-delivered meals, along with a decline in attendance at congregate sites. With regard to home-based care, state officials reported that Title III funding was not sufficient to meet the needs of those requiring assistance.

The GAO report estimated that 21% of people over 65 years needed transportation assistance in 2008. Those most likely in need of assistance were 80 years and older, female, and at or below the poverty level. More than a quarter of the agencies (26%) providing transportation were unable to meet all of the requests. Most trips were limited to quality-of-life activities, such as trips to senior centers or congregate meal sites (GAO, 2011).

Finally, the GAO report noted that 47% of the reporting agencies had reduced aging services budgets between 2009 and 2010. While funding decreased, requests for home-delivered meals, support services, and caregiver services increased. Agencies thus created waitlists, provided less service, searched for additional funds, or used Recovery Act funds as a temporary solution to meet the demands.

Indicators of OAA Effectiveness

The AOA remains concerned about the extent to which its many programs are reaching its intended population. The most recent data on the services provided by the AOA indicate that in 2010 over 11 million older persons and their caregivers (20% of the country's population over 60 years) were served (DHHS, 2012). Indicators show that it has been helping homebound elderly at risk of nursing home placement to stay at home, and it has increased its efficiency, in that it is serving the neediest in a cost-effective manner and has continued to build the capacity of state agencies and AAAs to implement comprehensive systems of care

(AOA, 2013). However, concerns remain that without increases in funding, it will be difficult to maintain performance. With declining state and local revenues, their required funding matches for programs are expected to decline.

In order to improve its performance, the AOA is focusing on improving efficiency, improving client outcomes, and further targeting services offered to the vulnerable elderly (ACL Congressional Justification, 2013). It has also adapted a new set of performance indicators that assess the quantity and quality of its services, including longitudinal and experimental methodology, thereby accurately assessing its effectiveness. It is also using new methods for measuring the impact of its services, including reducing the percentage of caregivers reporting trouble in obtaining services, using a nursing home predictor index, and increasing service use by the most vulnerable.

The OAA expired in 2011, and has not yet been reauthorized by Congress. Reauthorization would extend funding through 2018. The reauthorization bill would also strengthen protections against elder abuse, improve nutrition programs, modernize senior centers, improve family caregiver support, and give new focus to LGBT older adults and minorities (Bonamici, 2014). Without this reauthorization, the effectiveness of the Act in addressing the needs and rights of older adults is questionable.

SUMMARY

Both the White House Conferences on Aging and the OAA provide frameworks for addressing the major concerns and issues affecting older Americans. The history of each underscores both needs and rights as they promote the participation of older adults in the development of policies, empowering them within the society. The goals of each are to promote the well-being and independence of older persons and to help assure their security and participation in the community.

The White House Conference, with its emphasis on the involvement of older adults in the setting of policies, offers an important model for policy development. However, given this important role, a meeting has yet to be scheduled for 2015. The Health and Human Services budget requested $3,000,000 for the meeting; this sum was in the president's budget, but the money has not yet been appropriated (DHHS, 2014). Historically, the conferences have played major roles in setting the agenda for aging policies. With the rapidly aging population in the country and its increasing diversity, there is a pressing need for the conference to help assure that relevant policies may be developed.

The OAA, which both proposes and implements policies, must deal with many challenges. The role of older adults in the development of plans and services is supported through the mandate of the OAA that they comprise more than 50% of the members of local AAA advisory councils. On the state and local level, there is a wide disparity among programs and even in the focus of the policies (Hudson, 2010).

Accordingly, each geographic network serves local populations that differ in numbers and types of participants, budget constraints, and even their focus. Funding does not recognize these disparities and thus may be insufficient to meet an area's needs.

On the federal level, AOA's FY 2014 budget request for $2.1 billion means that the budget has changed little since its $1.9 billion allocated in 2013. Without increases in appropriations, it will be increasingly difficult to meet the costs associated with inflation or the growing number of older Americans needing services. Waiting lists and curtailed services can be expected to continue, seriously jeopardizing the programs' ability to fulfill the needs and sustain the rights of millions of older adults. The policies and programs are in place; the challenge is to effectively implement them.

QUESTIONS FOR DISCUSSION

1. Discuss some of the ways in which the White House Conference on Aging reflects human rights.
2. How are human rights highlighted in the OAA?
3. What is a key factor impeding the effectiveness of the OAA in meeting its goals?
4. If you were developing services for older adults to help them to remain in the community, what programs would you see as a priority?

REFERENCES

Administration on Aging. (2012a). *Nutrition services.* Retrieved from http://www.aoa.gov/AoA_programs/HCLTC/Nutrition_Services/index.aspx

Administration on Aging. (2012b). *Use of transportation services among OAA Title III Program Participants,* Research Brief No. 6. Washington, DC: Dept of HHS.

Administration on Aging. (2013). *National family caregiver support program.* Retrieved from http://www.aoa.gov/aoa_programs/hcltc/caregiver/index.aspx

Administration for Community Living. (2013). *Justification of estimates for appropriations Committee.* Retrieved from http://acl.gov/About_ACL/Budget/docs/FY_2013_AoA_CJ_Feb_2012.pdf

Altshuler, N., & Schimmel, J. (2010). *Aging in place: Do Older Americans Act Title III services reach those most likely to enter nursing homes?* Mathematica Policy Research Inc., Washington, DC.

Anderson, K., Dabelko-Schoeny, H., & Tarrant, S. (2012). A constellation of concerns: Exploring the present and the future challenges for adult day services. *Home Health Care Management Practice, 24*(3), 132–139.

Barrett, A., & Schimmel, J. (2010). *Multiple service use among OAA Title III Program Participants.* Issue Brief No. 3, Mathematica Policy Research, Inc., Washington, DC.

Bonamici, S. (2014). *Reauthorize Older Americans Act.* Retrieved from http://thehill.com/opinion/op-ed/200052-reauthorize-older-americans-act

Centers for Disease Control and Prevention, National Center for Health Statistics. (2012). *Long-term care services in the United States: 2013 overview.* Retrieved from http://www.cdc.gov/nchs/data/nsltcp/long_term_care_services_2013.pdf

Chen, Y., & Thompson, E. (2010). Understanding factors that influence success of home and community based services in keeping older adults in community settings. *Journal of Aging and Health, 22,* 267–275.

Department of Health and Human Services (DHHS), Administration on Aging. (2012). *FY online performance index.* Washington, DC: Author.

Department of Health and Human Services (DHHS). (2014). *HHS 2015 budget in brief.* Retrieved from http://www.hhs.gov/budget/fy2015-hhs-budget-in-brief/hhs-fy2015budget-in-brief-acl.html

Dichele, R. (2013*). Innovate or else: Challenges for the 21st century senior center.* Retrieved from http://www.asaging.org/blog/innovate-or-else-challenges-21st-century-senior-center

Foster, L., & Kleinman, R. (2011). *Supporting family caregivers through Title III of the OAA*. Administration on Aging, Research Brief No. 5. Washington, DC: Author.

Gitelson, R., Ho, C., Fitzpatrick, T., Case, A., & McCabe, J. (2008). The impact of senior centers on participants in congregate meal programs. *Journal of Park and Recreation Administration, 26*, 136–151.

Giunta, N. (2010). The national family caregiver support program: A multivariate examination of state-level implementation. *Journal of Aging & Social Policy, 22*, 249–266.

Godfrey, D. (2010). In search of adequate funding for legal assistance for low-income seniors. *Bifocal, 32*(1), 1–12.

Godfrey, D. (2012). Another look at the numbers: Legal services and Older Americans Act reauthorization. *Bifocal, 33*(4), 60–65.

Hanham, R. (1983). Aging in America: The White House conference of 1981 in retrospect. *American Journal of Public Health, 73*(7), 799–801.

Herrera, A., George, R., Angel, J., Markides, K., & Torres-Gil, F. (2013). Variation in older Americans Act caregiver service use, unmet hours of care and independence among Hispanics, African Americans, and Whites. *Home Health Care Services Quarterly, 32*(1), 35–56.

Hudson, R. (2010). *The new politics of old age policy*. Johns Hopkins Press: Baltimore.

Leary, M. (2007). *Draft final report for the evaluation of select consumer, program and system characteristics under the supportive service program (Title IIIB of the Older Americans Act)*. RTI Project Number 0208490.016007. Research Triangle Park.

Lee, J., Sinnett, S., Bengl, R., Johnson, M., & Brown, A. (2011). Unmet needs for the Older Americans Act Nutrition Program. *Journal of Applied Gerontology, 30*, 587–606.

McMillion, R. (2011). A problem of aging. *American Bar Association Journal, 97*(10), 62–62.

Metlife Mature Market Institute. (2010). *Market Survey of Long-term care costs*. Westport, Author.

National Association of State Units on Aging. (1982). *An orientation to the Older Americans Act*. Washington, DC: Author.

National Institute of Senior Centers. (2010). *Senior centers fact sheet*. Washington, DC: Author. Retrieved from http://www.ncoa.org/press-room/fact-sheets/senior-center-fact-sheet.html

Stoil, M. (2006). Should we retire the White House Conference on Aging? *Long-term Care Management, 55*(2), 12–14.

U.S. Senate Special Committee on Aging. (1971). *The Administration on Aging or a Successor? U.S. Government Printing Office.* Washington, DC.

United States Government Accounting Office. (2011). *Older Americans Act: More should be done to measure the extent need for services.* Washington, DC: Author.

United States Government Accounting Office. (2012). *Options to better target need and improve equity.* Washington, DC: Author.

White House Conference on Aging. (2005). *50 resolutions as voted by 2005 WHCOA delegates.* Washington, DC: Author.

CHAPTER 3

Income Policy and Human Rights

Having an adequate income in old age and the economic stability to maintain a decent standard of living are basic human rights (Universal Declaration of Human Rights [UNDHR], Articles 22 and 25). However, economic concerns are among the most pressing issues faced by many older Americans, whose economic solvency is often at risk.

POVERTY

The U.S. Census Bureau measures poverty by comparing pretax income against a threshold that is three times the cost of a minimum food diet. This threshold, set in 1963, is adjusted for family size and age of householder, but not for geographic region (U.S. Census, 2014c). The calculations do not include noncash benefits, such as food stamps or housing subsidies, nor consider expenditures, such as those on health care, which is a major part of older persons' budgets. In 2012, the poverty threshold for a household of two persons over the age of 65 was $13,892. Accordingly, 9% of persons over the age of 65 were in poverty in 2012, and 5.8% were considered near poor (up to 125% of the poverty level; U.S. Census, 2014b).

The Supplementary Poverty Measure (SPM) initiated in 2011 includes more resources, such as food stamps and tax credits, and deducts out-of-pocket medical and other necessary expenses in its calculations (U.S. Census, 2014c). Including the medical expenses in the measure accounted for a significant difference between the two measures of poverty as the SPM showed a higher poverty rate (14.8%) for those over 65, with older people spending a large part of their income on health care (U.S. Census, 2014a).

Further research on the SPM finds nearly half (48%) of those over 65 years to be economically vulnerable (Gould & Cooper, 2013). People over 80 years, women, Blacks, and Hispanics were the most vulnerable. Important in their findings is the comparison of poverty rate among married White men (3.1%) with that of older Black women (36.5%) and older Hispanic women (40.5%).

SOCIAL SECURITY

Social Security, established in 1935, is an insurance program intended to protect individuals and their families from earnings loss due to retirement, disability, or death. The benefits that it provides were intended to be a supplement to other incomes and not a sole source or a replacement. All employees, regardless of their salaries, pay contributions through a payroll tax of 6.2%, up to a taxable maximum of $117,000 in 2014. Persons earning more than the maximum do not pay a higher tax rate of contribution (Social Security Administration [SSA], 2014a). Benefits are increased annually in order to keep up with inflation as determined by the Consumer Price Index. Social Security is a universal benefit, in that it covers almost every American.

Retirement benefits are available to those who have been employed for at least 10 years and have paid into the system. Persons can begin taking benefits at the age of 62 or wait until their full retirement age of either 66 or 67. Those taking early benefits receive a lesser amount that will remain constant. Postponing receiving benefits to beyond age 62 to 66 or 67 is often advantageous with regard to the returns, particularly for those who do not have any other source of retirement income. People with lower earnings than their spouse can often receive benefits equal to half the spouse's benefit while the spouse is alive, as long as they have been married for at least 10 years. Widows of a retired beneficiary and children are also eligible for benefits.

Social Security is the primary source of income for older minority Americans as fewer people in these groups have private pensions while also having low retirement savings. One-third of older African Americans and Hispanics depend on Social Security for more than 90% of their total income (Koenig & Waid, 2012). In comparison to nearly half (48%) of older nonminority Americans who receive Social Security, one-third of older African Americans, 22% of older Hispanics, and 29% of older Asians receive it. Moreover, in 2011, the median annual benefit received by older White beneficiaries was $13,577 in comparison to $11,957 for African Americans and $10,757 for Hispanics (Koenig & Waid, 2012).

Social Security benefits are regressive, in that they replace a higher proportion of the earnings of low-income earners. However, because Whites have generally had higher lifetime earnings than minorities, they have higher benefits. Consequently, low-income minority persons remain at risk for poverty.

Among the suggestions to increase the economic status of these older adults are providing individuals with long lifetime work histories but low earnings enhanced benefits, as well as credits for caregiving and, where applicable, poor health status (Favreault, 2010).

Offering a minimum benefit would improve the adequacy and equitability of the system as it would ensure that those who had spent years working and contributing would have sufficient benefits at retirement. Other suggestions include strengthening the Cost of Living Adjustment (COLA) and increasing benefits (National Committee to Preserve Social Security and Medicare, 2014).

WOMEN AND SOCIAL SECURITY

In 1935 when Social Security was established, women's traditional roles were to be homemakers while men were the breadwinners, and divorce was not common. Today, these roles have changed. Women 65 years and older are likely to have had substantial work histories, and also to have contributed to the Social Security system; however, these contributions do not necessarily relate to any additional benefits.

Women receive benefits either through their own employment or through the employment of their spouse. Their own benefits are available at their retirement, while spousal benefits are paid either when their spouse retires or reaches full retirement age. If the wife's benefit is equal or greater than that of the spouse, she receives only her own. If the spouse's benefit is greater, she receives her own and enough of the spouse's to bring the total up to the higher benefit.

As the benefits that male retired workers receive are substantially higher than those of female retirees, over a quarter of women receiving retired worker benefits also receive benefits from their spouses (SSA, 2013). At the same time, those receiving spouse-only benefits declined from 33% in 1960 to 10% in 2010, while those receiving retired worker benefits on their contributions rose from 29% in 1960 to 46% in 2010 (SSA, 2013). Consequently, the proportion of women receiving benefits based on their own earning is increasing.

Spouse benefits are most valuable for couples when one has a continued history of contributions and the other has none. It has no value for couples where the covered earnings of each are equal. The majority of women claim benefits at the earliest age, 62 years, and only 18% wait until their normal retirement age (U.S. Government Accounting Office [GAO], 2012).

The spousal benefit is not available for women who never married and women who divorce before 10 years of marriage. These factors have strong effects on minority groups whose marriage rates are less than those of Whites. Since the overturning of the Defense of Marriage Act, spouses in same-sex partnerships or marriages may be entitled to benefits, even in states in which they are not recognized.

Social Security benefits constitute 90% of the family income for women 65 years and older. These women are also less likely than their male peers to have income from other pensions; if they do, the median pension is lower. In addition, as women live longer than their spouse, they are more likely to outlive any retirement savings. The economic vulnerability of older women is magnified by divorce and widowhood, which can be financially devastating (GAO, 2012). Overall, the lower average earnings, higher life expectancy, and lower Social Security benefits of women contribute to their high rates of poverty in their later years.

Supplemental Security Income

Supplemental Security Income (SSI) is a federal income supplement program funded through general revenues that is available for older, blind, and disabled people who meet certain income guidelines. It is the main source of cash assistance for older people in poverty. The program was initiated in 1974 to replace federal-state assistance programs, Aid to the Elderly, Aid to the Permanently and Totally Disabled, and Aid to the Blind. SSI is administered through Social Security Administration. Legal immigrants are eligible for benefits.

Eligibility is based on income: individuals with less than $2,000 in resources or a couple with less than $3,000. For 2014, the maximum annual benefit for an individual is $8,657, and for a couple $12,984 (SSA, 2014a). Most states supplement SSI using the same federal formula for eligibility. About 25% of the recipients are 65 years or older, receiving an average monthly payment of $430 (SSA, 2014b). These recipients are also very poor, with nearly 70% in the bottom fifth of the national income distribution of all persons over 65 years.

Although SSI can provide the needed income for the elderly, their participation in the program has always been limited and has continued to decline, while there has been a concomitant growth in SSI participation on the basis of disability (Center on Budget and Policy Priorities, 2013). The decline in participation by older adults is attributed to increases in Social Security benefits and restrictions on legal immigrants who arrived after 1996 (Center on Budget and Policy Priorities, 2013). Moreover, Social Security raised 14.5 million elderly Americans above the poverty line in 2011, which made them ineligible for SSI payments (Van de Water & Sherman, 2012).

Another barrier to the participation of older adults in SSI is the asset level limits of $2,000 and $3,000, which has not increased since 1989. More older adults might qualify if indexing is adjusted to inflation. Similarly, income limits may also impact eligibility. The 2014 limits of $721 for an individual and $1,082 for a married couple mean that many do not qualify but are still poor. A 2002 study by the SSA found that increasing the amount of income that persons could have would raise participation by the elderly by 20% and decrease the elderly poverty gap by 8% (Davies, 2002).

45

Supplemental Nutrition Assistance Program

In 2012, 15.3% of those over 60 years were at risk of hunger (Zilak & Gunderson, 2014). The people most at risk were those living in the South and Southwest, those who were racial or ethnic minorities, those with lower incomes, and those between 60 and 69 years. From 2001 to 2012, the percentage of older adults facing hunger increased by 44%, with nearly two out of three having incomes above the poverty line (Zilak & Gunderson, 2014). Hunger and malnutrition contribute to poor health and diminished well-being.

The Supplemental Nutrition Assistance Program (SNAP) was initiated in 2008 as a means of restructuring the food stamp program that began in 1964. The SNAP program places greater emphasis on nutrition than the original program. Fourteen percent of the total population receives SNAP assistance, with approximately 19% of the recipients being seniors (Center on Budget and Policy Priorities, 2013). Moreover, nearly 90% of the households receiving benefits include an older person. In 2010, the average benefit was $144 for seniors (www.snaptohealth. org). However, funding for the program remains precarious as it is tied to other federal funding reductions. With the current benefits barely adequate to meet the costs of food, further cuts could be disastrous for many in the low-income category, which would severely impact their right for an adequate standard of living.

Eligibility is based on household income, although those on SSI are categorically eligible; however, they usually have to complete a SNAP application. The income criteria for a person 60 years and older are 100% of the federal poverty level. However, older adults are able to deduct medical expenses of $35 per month as well as rent and mortgage payments. Resource limits are decided by the states but do not include the home that the older adult is living in. Applicants need to submit documents verifying their eligibility and often have to appear in person.

Participation by older persons in the SNAP program is low and they remain underserved (Center on Budget and Policy Priorities, 2013). Data from 2010 have revealed that only 35% of persons over 65 years who were eligible for the program participated. At the same time, those being served by the program are in need. In 2011, 68% of the elderly participants were in poverty, 72% were in one-person households, and 40% were in households receiving SSI.

The lack of participation by older persons in the program has been attributed to many factors (Food Research and Action Center, 2013). Many believe that they will get only the minimum benefit and most are often unaware of their eligibility. This lack of knowledge is related to the fact that they are less likely to be living with others who have received food stamps previously or to know anyone who has received them. Stigma also plays a role in their nonparticipation. Persons report that they would feel embarrassed if others knew that they were receiving food stamps; they were also concerned about being perceived negatively by merchants. The application process itself can be confusing, particularly for those who are not English-speaking. Waiving the requirement for in-office applications and reducing complicated verification requirements could also help increase participation.

Findings from a demonstration program that focused on increasing elderly or working poor participation in SNAP found that educating people about the SNAP and targeting efforts to potential participants were important (Mathematica Policy Research, 2014). In addition, simplifying the application process by offering direct assistance with applications as well as waiving the necessity of having to apply in person were particularly important strategies for enrolling seniors.

Low-Income Energy Assistance Program

The Low-Income Home Energy Assistance Program (LIHEAP) is a federal block grant to states that help them to operate home energy assistance programs for low-income households. The program helps eligible persons—those with incomes lower than 150% of the poverty level or 60% of the state median income—pay heating and/or cooling bills. It also funds low-cost weatherization projects and helps with energy-related emergencies.

LIHEAP was last reauthorized in 2005. However, limited funds permit states to grant assistance only to the most eligible households. Without increases in funding that realistically meet the utility expenditures of low-income elderly, the program's ability to meet their needs is compromised. Bills to increase funding in 2014 did not pass and funding for FY 2015 at $3.39 billion is well below the 2010 level of $5.1 billion. Consequently, the ability of the program to meet the home fuel needs of many is uncertain (Electric Cooperative Association [ECT], 2014).

Thirty percent of older households have income less than $20,000, which and is considered as the greatest energy burden (Jackson & Walters, 2013). More than half of these older households use natural gas as their primary heating source, and the assistance that LIHEAP offers is not sufficient to meet its rising costs. The program is particularly important for persons over the age of 65 who have the highest expenditures for utilities as a proportion of their overall expenditures; those living alone and minorities having the highest spending ratios (Walters, 2013).

Private Pensions

Private pensions are a major factor in reducing poverty among older Americans. There are basically two types of pensions: defined benefit (DB) and defined contribution (DC). Pensions with DB guarantee income after retirement that continues until death, with the surviving spouse having access to all or part of it. The Pension Benefit Guarantee Corporation (PBGC) guarantees these pensions. Older people with these pensions are less likely to be reliant on public assistance such as SSI and are less likely to experience hardships with regard to food, health care, and shelter.

The DC plans are usually tax-deferred accounts to which employees and their employers make a DC. The accumulated funds are available to workers at retirement. If they leave for other employment, many plans permit rollovers into Individual Retirement Accounts (IRA). The amount of money in DC and IRA plans increased sixfold between 1990 and 2011, while that in DB plans doubled (Board of Governors of the Federal Reserve System, 2012). Persons enrolled in DC plans increased from 40% in 1989 to 51% in 2012 (Wiatrowski, 2011).

The risk of poverty increases by 50% for older Americans without a pension (Porell & Oakley, 2012). Findings based on data from the

U.S. Census Bureau's Survey of Income Program Participation (SIPP) indicate that the rate of poverty for older households without a pension with a DB was nine times greater than the rate for those with a DB—an increase that was six times greater than the rate in 2010 (Porell & Oakley, 2012).

These pensions protect the middle-class from falling into poverty upon retirement. Equally important is that DB pensions protect those who are most economically vulnerable—minorities and women—in their retirement years. Unfortunately, these groups are the least likely to be covered by any pension plan or to have invested in a plan due to shorter and more interrupted work histories. Data from 2009 indicate that a majority (64.6%) of White workers were covered by a pension plan in comparison to 55.7% of Black workers and 38.4% of Hispanics (Butrica & Johnson, 2010). Moreover, Black and Hispanic workers were significantly less likely than Whites to participate when employers offered pension plans. At the same time, fewer employers today are offering such plans. In the 1980s 39% of private employers offered pensions, whereas in 2009 only 15% offered pensions (Employee Benefit Research Institute, 2011). Half of all Americans do not have a workplace retirement plan (Oakley & Kenneally, 2013).

DB pensions are more protective of retirement security than DC plans, which often invest in financial markets that can be very volatile. Additionally, persons can often borrow against these DC accounts, which means that they may have fewer savings for retirement. Most DB plans, although offering retirees some financial security, are not adjusted to reflect inflation and so their actual worth may be less than the benefits received from a well-managed DC account. However, in a review on the impact of the DB and DC programs on the most financially vulnerable, Wolff (2011) reports that minorities, workers with less than a college education, women, and young workers with a DC plan are less well-off than those with DB pensions in terms of retirement income and replacement of preretirement income.

Although DB pension plans can be important in securing economic well-being in retirement, the number of companies offering them has declined along with the number of workers who are covered. In 1975, 88% of private sector workers had DB coverage, with the percentage dropping to 33% in 2005 (Munnell, Haverstick, & Soto, 2007). Reasons for the decline in plans include increased regulation, changes in industry with fewer unionized jobs, and a lack of knowledge of employee preference for traditional DB plans (Boivie, 2012). At the same time, shifting from a DB to a DC plan does not decrease funding requirements for employers, although it can increase the retirement costs for employees.

The majority of public pensions, those provided by state and local governments, are DB plans that have given employees a sense of security for their retirement. However, as state and local governments continue to confront fiscal shortages, many find that they are having difficulties fulfilling their benefit obligations. Many of these plans are underfunded, meaning that contributions must be increased with the increased risk of reduced retirement benefits. As these pensions are not covered by the PBGC, cities, even if insolvent, may be required to meet their final obligations to retirees.

States are unable to claim bankruptcy. However, the gap between what states owe in pension benefits and existent funding continues to increase (Pew Charitable Trusts, 2014). Consequently, in order to maintain current pension programs, states may move away from DB schemes to DCs, reduced benefits, and increased contributions (Beerman, 2013).

Veterans

Since the colonial era, the United States has provided special benefits and allowances for veterans. These continue to this day through veterans' pensions offered through the Department of Veterans Affairs (VA). Persons who have served 20 years in the military can receive 50% of their monthly base pay at retirement. An additional 2.5% is allotted for each year served over 20 years to a maximum of 100% of their pay with 40 years of service.

Supplemental pensions are available to those who have served in a war. The veteran must have had at least 90 days of active service duty with at least one day during a wartime period. These benefits are available for those 65 years or older; those disabled or in nursing homes; or those receiving SSI. Assets are also counted in determining eligibility. In contrast to programs such as SSI, the VA considers medical expenses against income, thereby reducing the amount of countable income. Survivors of deceased veterans are eligible for survivor benefits.

Veterans and their spouses who are eligible for pensions may also be eligible for Aid and Attendance or Housebound benefits, which increase the annual amount they receive. This benefit has a higher income limit so that even those who may be ineligible for the pension may still receive the benefit. Eligibility depends on requiring assistance with activities of daily living or being housebound or in a nursing home.

SUMMARY

Having adequate income that permits older persons to live securely and with dignity is a fundamental human right. Policies in the United States are cognizant of this right and have adopted many policies with regard to income security. However, the effectiveness of these policies in securing the rights of the most vulnerable remains dubious as the policies fall short of making real differences in their lives.

Fundamental to improving the economic status of older Americans is a more accurate measure of poverty. The present poverty measure is outdated and does not reflect the actual situation and challenges confronting many subgroups of elderly. The assumption that older people have fewer expenses than younger ones coupled with not allowing for their health expenditures invalidates the reliability of the current poverty measure and means that many must go without access to programs that might assist them.

Social Security remains the foundation of retirement income for older Americans and, although it was always intended to be a supplement in retirement, for the most vulnerable it is their primary source of income. For many of these retirees and their spouses, who spent a lifetime in low-salary jobs, the benefits that they receive are not sufficient to lift them out of poverty. Increasing the earnings replacement rate of benefits so that they are more commensurate with earnings could increase their adequacy.

As discussed, women who are among the most dependent on Social Security remain among the most vulnerable to poverty in their later years. Adjustments that take into account their interrupted work histories and lifetimes of lower wages would benefit many of these older recipients. Understanding the gender gap that pervades the program could assist many to stay out of poverty.

Strengthening and assuring the solvency of the system should not be based on punishing those who need it most. Curtailing benefits and denying cost of living increases will continue to impact the most vulnerable older people while having much less effect on the wealthier beneficiaries. Assuring a minimum Social Security benefit for retired workers could further protect their financial security and thus sustain their right to an adequate income.

The SSI program, designed to assist low-income persons, could go further in meeting its goals. Increasing the asset limits that people are able to have, raising the benefits, and increasing participation so that more elderly are enrolled could protect the ability of many older persons to live comfortably in the community. It is equally important to assure that older immigrants have greater access to the program. Continuing to limit eligibility to those entering before 1996 will keep many older persons in poverty. Moreover, it is critical that the access of older ethnic persons is increased through outreach that enables them to understand the program and facilitates their application and participation. In order to increase the effectiveness of the program in addressing poverty among the elderly, benefits could be more adequate so that they actually take people out of poverty rather than just reduce it. This involves raising and indexing the asset and income limits. In addition, SSI eligibility could be extended to immigrants who have been left out of the system since 1996.

Programs such as SNAP and LIHEAP have the potential to assist the most economically vulnerable by providing them with nutritional support and assistance with their utilities. The policies are in place but each is limited by a lack of sufficient resources. In addition, it is troubling that only a minority of those eligible for SNAP actually participate. However, their full participation would surely outpace the ability of the program to sufficiently meet the nutritional needs of low-income elderly.

Retirement pensions are critically essential to economic solvency for older persons. Those with pensions continue to fare better than their peers who do not have them. Again, it is the most vulnerable of the elderly—women and minorities—who are the least likely to have a pension. With pensions playing significant roles in the lives of older persons, plans should be strengthened and expanded to include the participation of those groups that tended to be ignored. Unfortunately, the number of companies offering pensions continues to decline and many plans, both public and private, are seriously underfunded and challenged in meeting their obligations to their current or future retirees. Given the major role these pension schemes play in protecting the economic well-being of many retirees, strategies to strengthen and expand them need to be developed to ensure that the rights of these employees are met.

Finally, it is difficult for persons to save for retirement if during their working years they are struggling to survive on low wages that keep them barely above the poverty level. Without helping to assure the solvency of persons in their younger years, it is difficult to assure income adequacy in their later years.

QUESTIONS FOR DISCUSSION

1. Discuss the role of Social Security in the lives of older people. How does it relate to human rights?
2. What are some of the major concerns about private pensions? Describe the differences between DB and DC pension schemes and which you think is preferable.
3. What are some of the reasons that women are at risk with regards to Social Security?
4. How would you strengthen the retirement income of older adults?

REFERENCES

Beerman, J. (2013). The public pension crisis. *Washington and Lee Law Review*, 70(1), 3–94.

Boivie, I. (2012). *Measuring the economic impact of DB pension expenditures*. National Institute of Retirement Security. Washington, DC: Author.

Butrica, B., & Johnson, R. (2010). *Racial, ethnic and gender differentials in employer-sponsored pensions*. Washington, DC: Urban Institute.

Center on Budget and Policy Priorities. (2013). *Chart book: SNAP helps struggling families put food on the table*. Washington, DC: Author.

Davies, P. (2002). Modeling SSI financial eligibility and simulating the effect of policy options. *Social Security Bulletin, 64*(2).

Electric Cooperative Association (ECT). (2014). *LIHEAP funding short of supporter's goal*. Retrieved from http://www.ect.coop/public-policy-watch/legislation/liheap-funding-short-of-supporters-goal/71109

Employee Benefit Research Institute. (2011). *FAQs about benefit retirement issues*. Washington, DC: Author.

Favreault, M. (2010). *Workers with low Social Security benefits: Implications for reform*, policy briefs. Washington, DC: Urban Institute.

Food Research and Action Center. (2013). *Seniors and SNAP/food stamps*. Washington, DC: Author.

GAO. (2012). *Retirement security, women still face challenges, report to the Chairman, Special Committee on Aging*. Washington, DC: U.S. Senate.

Gould, E., & Cooper, D. (2013). *Financial security of elderly Americans at risk: Proposed changes to Social Security and Medicare could make a majority of seniors economically vulnerable*, Briefing Paper 362. Economic Policy Institute.

Jackson, A., & Walters, N. (2013). *Winter heating costs for older and low-income households*. Washington, DC: AARP Public Policy Institute.

Koenig, G., & Waid, M. (2012). *Social Security: A key retirement income source for older minorities*. Public Policy Institute, AARP. Washington, DC: AARP.

Mathematica Policy Research. (2014). *Reaching the underserved elderly and working poor in SNAP: Valuation findings from the fiscal year 2009 pilots, final report*. Retrieved from http://www.mathematica-mpr.com/~/media/publications

Munnell, A., Haverstick, K., & Soto, M. (2007). *Why have defined benefit plans survived in the public sector? State and local pension plans*. Chestnut Hill, MA: Center for Retirement Research at Boston College.

National Committee to Preserve Social Security and Medicare. (2014). *Boost Social Security now*. Retrieved from http://www.ncpssm.org/Portals/0/pdf/boost-ss-viewpoint.pdf

Oakley, D., & Kenneally, K. (2013). *Pensions and retirement savings*. Washington, DC: National Institute on Retirement Security.

Pew Charitable Trusts. (2014). *The fiscal health of state pension plans funding gap continues to grow*. Retrieved from http://www.pewtrusts.org/en/

research-and-analysis/analysis/2014/04/08/the-fiscal-health-of-state-pension-plans-funding-gap-continues-to-grow

Porell, F., & Oakley, D. (2012). *The pension factor 2012; the role of defined benefit pensions in reducing elder economic hardships.* Washington, DC: National Institute on Retirement Security.

SSA. (2013). *Women's eligibility basis for Social Security retirement benefits is changing.* Retrieved from http://www.socialsecurity.gov/retirementpolicy/research/womens-eligibility.html

SSA. (2014a). *Research, statistics, & policy analysis.* Retrieved from http://www.ssa.gov/policy/docs/ssb/v64n2/v64n2p16.pdf

SSA. (2014b). *SSI federal payment amounts for 2014.* Retrieved from http://www.ssa.gov/oact/cola/SSI.html

U.S. Census. (2014a). *Experimental measures: Supplemental poverty measure overview.* Retrieved from https://www.census.gov/hhes/povmeas/methodology/supplemental/overview.html

U.S. Census. (2014b). *Facts for figures, older Americans month.* Retrieved from http://www.census.gov/newsroom/releases/archives/facts_for_features_special_editions/cb14-ff07.html

U.S. Census. (2014c). *How the Census Bureau measures poverty.* Retrieved from https://www.census.gov/hhes/www/poverty/about/overview/measure.html

Van de Water, P., & Sherman, A. (2012). *Social Security keeps 21 million Americans out of poverty: A state by state analysis.* Washington, DC: Center on Budget and Policy Priorities.

Walters, N. (2013). *An analysis of 2011 utility expenditures by older consumers.* Public Policy Institute, AARP. Washington, DC.

Wiatrowski, W. J. (2011). *Changing landscape of employer based retirement benefits.* Washington, DC: U.S. Department of Labor. Retrieved from http://www.bls.gov/opub/cwc/print/cm20110927ar01p1.htm.

Wolff, E. (2011). *The transformation of the American pension system: Was it beneficial for workers.* Michigan: Upjohn Institute for Employment Research.

Zilak, J., & Gunderson, C. (2014). *The state of senior hunger in America 2012: An annual report,* prepared for the National Foundation to End Senior Hunger. Washington, DC: National Foundation to End Senior Hunger.

CHAPTER 4

Policy and the Right to Liberty and Security

Everyone has the right to "life, liberty, and security of person" (Universal Declaration of Human Rights [UNDHR], Article 3). The broad scope of these rights impacts many aspects of the lives of older adults, as society is responsible for the support that permits their realization. For many, particularly those with increasing impairments and declining resources, the possibility to have these rights met is extremely negligible; indeed, their very ability to remain at liberty in the community is at risk. A program that can seriously imperil these rights is that of guardianship.

GUARDIANSHIP

The right to life, liberty, and security is most profoundly challenged by guardianship, which is a procedure that can severely constrict the older adult's ability to act on his or her own and according to that individual's own wishes. Guardianship deems a person incompetent in making decisions on his or her own behalf. Based on the doctrine of *parens patriae*, "father of his country," states are given the right and duty to protect those persons unable to care for themselves and their property. This principle is enacted through the process of guardianship by which individuals judged to be incompetent and thus vulnerable and unable to act on behalf of their own best interests are assigned legal guardians by the court.

The Uniform Adult Guardianship and Protected Proceedings Jurisdiction Act (UAGPPJA) of 2007 attempts to improve the guardianship process by making it more uniform across states, and it is particularly important when a guardianship involves several states. It also offers procedures for appointing guardians and conservators, and strengthens the protection of those subjected to the proceedings while also seeking to balance the protection of the individual with the power of the guardian (Center for Elders and Courts, 2014).

Policy governing guardianship is designed and implemented at the state level; therefore, many variations exist regarding its implementation. The guardian is appointed by the court to make decisions for a person whom the court has judged to be incompetent in terms of self-care or money and estate management.

Basically, there are two forms of guardianship: guardianship of the ward, in which the guardian is responsible for all aspects of the individual's life; and guardianship of the estate, where the guardian is responsible only for money and property. Underlying both is the assumption that the guardian will act in the "best interests" of the person.

State laws specify the actions that guardians can make on their own and those that require prior court approval. Guardianship can be requested by anyone, and in most states attorneys file a request with the probate court. The ward is entitled to legal representation at the hearing. In order to terminate a guardianship, the individual must demonstrate to the court his or her ability to make decisions. Once granted, guardianship is seldom revoked.

Other less-restrictive alternatives to safeguarding the interests of the older person are conservatorship and power of attorney. Conservatorship is a process whereby an individual asks the probate court to appoint a conservator to manage the property and finances of the older person. The court must find the person able to make this decision to have a conservator but unable to manage financial affairs. Power of attorney gives the agent the power to make decisions such as medical, financial, or placement on the ward's behalf. The person must be mentally competent in order to create a power of attorney. However, the power of attorney may be made without any competency assessment; therefore, an older person lacking judgment could be persuaded to give power of attorney to a person who could subsequently exploit him or her.

In addition, there are few regulations regarding court-appointed attorneys acting as guardians or conservators. As monitoring of the work of these guardians is not routinely made, there is little control of their roles or performance with much scope for abuse. Consequently, there are few safeguards for the older person whose estate depends upon the integrity and ethics of this guardian.

A further concern regarding guardianship and the rights of the impaired older adult is that the evaluation of competency in one area does not necessarily coincide with other aspects of decision making. An individual may be unable to make a medical decision but is perfectly capable of functioning adequately at home. However, full, rather than a limited, guardianship restricted to only one aspect of decision making is usually granted. Moreover, there is no standardized uniform assessment for measuring competency, so there is much variation among jurisdictions. Comprehensive medical assessments involving a history of the individual's previous behaviors, medications, or physical conditions that could influence a person's capacity are rarely required. In addition, physicians making the assessment are not necessarily knowledgeable or trained to evaluate the capacity of the person to do tasks such as managing finances, driving, or even voting (Moye & Naik, 2011).

Guardianship rests on the assumption that the appointed guardian will act in the interest of, and according to the perceived wishes of, their ward. The problem is that there are few guarantees to assure that these assumptions are upheld. Moreover, even with the best intentions, family members may not make decisions in accordance with the wishes of their relative. In addition, their own emotional and financial burdens may intervene in their treatment or care decisions. Basic to the protection of the interests of the older adult are the interactions within the family. Wood & O'Bryan (2012) make the following suggestions to improve the guardianship system by helping to avoid unnecessary guardianship and strengthening accountability:

1. Develop mechanisms to assess elder abuse cases collaboratively for options that are less restrictive than guardianship. This would involve

multidisciplinary teams that screen and evaluate functional abilities and offer ways to limit guardianship or connect with needed services.

2. Provide training to guardians, particularly family guardians.

3. Consider criminal background checks as well as other sanctioned information on potential guardians.

4. Do active court monitoring of guardians to ensure the welfare of vulnerable older adults.

5. Improve guardian accountability.

Until these recommendations are passed, the fundamental rights of many older adults for life and liberty are in jeopardy.

LIVING IN THE COMMUNITY

The right to own property and to not be arbitrarily deprived of it is a basic human right (UNDHR, Article 17). In addition, the Madrid International Plan of Action on Ageing (United Nations, 2002) calls upon governments to improve the care and support of older persons as they need it (Article 6) and offer support that promotes their independence through supportive environments (Article 14).

The United States formally recognized the importance of supportive communities to older adults through its Community Innovations for Aging in Place Initiative (CIAIP) funded between 2009 and 2012. The program offered grants to localities that would help them in determining various developing strategies that would assist older adults to age in place. The services included care management, evidence-based disease prevention and health promotion programs education, socialization, recreation, and civic engagement opportunities (CIAIP, 2014). Grantees were required to collaborate with other community agencies and foundations in the development of services. Among the programs developed were a program of elder assistance for rural elderly, services for at-risk elders, and a pilot for building lifelong communities. Projects were required to describe the challenges that they faced and their plans for sustaining programs. Consequently, although no longer funded, CIAIP offers models for community programs focused on maintaining the most vulnerable older adults in the community.

AGING IN PLACE

Research indicates that aging in place is preferred by most older adults (AARP, 2005; Wagner, Shubair, & Michalos, 2010). It refers to the ability of persons to grow old in their own homes, staying as independent as possible, with an emphasis on using environmental modification to compensate for limitations and disabilities (Alley, Liebig, Pynoos, Banerjee, & Choi, 2007). These modifications frequently depend on community interventions and services that are not necessarily available, consequently compromising their rights to liberty and security.

Among the major environmental factors required to enable older persons to age in the community are zoning and infrastructure changes that allow them to remain connected to the community, a range of transportation and mobility options, and a variety of housing supports and choices (AARP, 2005). As functional competency declines, the importance of the environment to well-being increases (Lawton, 1980). Without adjustments and support, the environment often becomes unmanageable.

Housing

Between 2000 and 2010, the housing conditions of older Americans significantly declined (AARP, 2011). The recession depleted the equity in houses while costs increased, particularly for those with mortgages and low incomes. These individuals face continued increases in real estate taxes, which places an undue burden on older adults whose incomes tend to decline with age.

Consequently, older persons are more likely to spend more than half their income on housing. Whereas one in six households headed by persons younger than 65 years pay at least half their income to housing costs, this increases to one in four households headed by someone 85 years and older (Center for Housing Policy, 2012). These homeowners

61

are also more likely to be disabled and live in homes built before 1970, which often need significant repairs.

The housing burden is not confined to homeowners. Renters also struggle as they spend an even higher proportion of their income on housing. Among renters, 70% pay more than 30% of their income on rent, with 40% paying more than 50% (Commerce Department, 2008). Moreover, approximately 13 million low-income persons over the age of 50 years cannot afford their housing costs and/or live in inadequate housing (U.S. Department of Housing and Urban Development [HUD], 2014).

PROVISIONS FOR STAYING AT HOME

One of the fundamental requirements for remaining at home is living in an environment that is manageable. Independence in the community is predicated upon living in an environment that is compatible with the individual's functional status and is both compensatory of their limitations and supportive of their abilities.

Home Modifications

Home modifications are changes that are made to homes in order to make them more accessible and appropriate for persons with disabilities or older adults who have difficulties in physical functioning. By facilitating the ability of persons to deal with their immediate environment, modifications may potentially lower the decline of further functional impairment and thus even reduce medical costs and the risk of institutionalization (Liu & Lapane, 2009; Wahl, Fange, Oswald, Gitlin, & Iwarson, 2009). For many older people, modifying their home may be more cost-effective and desirable than moving (Koppen, 2009).

Housing modifications include ramps for entry, railings within the home, bathroom adjustments, kitchen modifications, elevators or lifts, and widening doorways. The costs of such modifications vary and for many are unaffordable (Freedman & Agree, 2008). However, funding to assist persons with home modifications remains limited.

There is some funding available under Title III of the Older Americans Act, which is distributed through the local Area Agencies on Aging (AAAs). Moreover, the waiver funds of Medicaid Home and Community-Based Services, as well as some Medicare funds, although primarily for health care, may also be used for home modifications.

States, through tax credits to homeowners, can assist in funding modifications that make houses more accessible. Local governments can use a portion of block grants, Community Development Block Grant and HOME Investment Partnerships, administered by the HUD, to help fund home modification programs. In addition, various non-profit groups offer assistance to elderly homeowners through the use of volunteers. But despite these sources of possible assistance, approximately 80% of home modifications are paid directly by the homeowners (National Association of Home Builders, 2011). Consequently, with this heavy dependence on private funds and limited availability of public funds, low-income elderly remain the least likely to be able to make the needed modifications.

Assistive Technology

Home adaptations are not limited to only structural or assistive devices. The growing application of technology to the needs of older adults has produced many devices that can make the home more support-ive. Telephones, one of the most common technological devices to be found in the home, can be particularly vital to older impaired persons. Telephones link them with services as well as with social contacts, but using a telephone can be challenging for many. Vision impairment can make it difficult to read numbers, mobility problems can make it diffi-cult to answer the phone, arthritis can affect the person's ability to dial and hold the receiver, and hearing impairments can act as barriers to hearing the ring or the other person.

Advancements in telecommunications have addressed many of the problems encountered by older persons. Telephones can be equipped with amplifiers and speakers that increase the volume of the ring and the voice, large numbers and letters are available to assist with dialing, while cordless phones can be important for those with mobility limitations. Telephones with memories that allow numbers to be dialed by pushing only one button, and some that even include pictures of the person to be called, can facilitate use by those with physical and even cognitive impairments.

Personal emergency response systems are devices that can attend to emergencies, such as falls, which might happen in the home. They can provide a sense of security to persons living alone and their caregivers. The system includes a small radio transmitter, worn as a bracelet or around the neck, which transmits a telephone signal to a 24-hour emergency center when help is needed. The person does not need to be at home to make the transmission. Systems are also available that automatically call the person if no activity has been noted in a particular period of time. The response centers may be in hospitals or in private companies. Local persons identified by the user—such as friends, relatives, or a formal agency—are immediately contacted by the response center as soon as an emergency signal is received.

Monitoring systems involve small wireless sensors placed throughout the house that track movements and even learn daily activity patterns. This will notify others if some unusual activity occurs such as a fall or no waking up. Systems are also available that dispense medications and provide reminders and notifications if a medicine is not taken. However, these systems are expensive and are not covered by government subsidies.

As the century begins and innovations in technology continue to be developed, the scope of devices that can assist the impaired elderly by enabling them to remain independent continues to expand. As well as giving persons relief, assistive technology is important, in that it can also foster the person's sense of control and self-confidence.

Some limited coverage may be provided under Medicare or Medicaid if the devices are primarily for a medical purpose. Under the Medicaid Waiver, most states will reimburse for personal emergency response systems but funding for other services is very limited. However, other sources of government funding have yet to be developed, meaning that these programs are not affordable to many who could desperately use them.

Reverse Mortgages

Reverse mortgages permit older homeowners to convert part of the equity in their home into cash. The person sells the house to the lender, who then gives him or her monthly payments, which continue as long as they live in the home. The loan is repaid when the person dies, sells the home, or the home is no longer the primary residence.

There are three types of mortgages. Single purpose mortgages are usually for home repairs or improvements. Persons with low or moderate incomes qualify for these mortgages. Home Equity Conversion Mortgages (HECMs) that are backed by the HUD are more expensive with higher costs but can be used for any purpose and have no income or medical requirements. Proprietary reverse mortgages are private loans backed by companies.

Applicants must prove that they are good risks for the loans and that they can make their property tax and homeowner's insurance payments. Financial assessments may also include credit histories that potentially could make getting such loans more difficult for low-income persons who may not have much credit. For persons who appear "risky," a portion of their reverse mortgage proceeds will be used to cover property taxes and homeowner's insurance.

Although generally helpful, there are several factors that need to be considered when seeking a reverse mortgage. There may be fees and costs associated with the loans; in addition, the amount owed on the mortgage increases with time as the interest on the outstanding balance is added to the amount owed each month. Most mortgages also have variable interest rates, and the interest on reverse mortgages is not tax deductible until the loan is paid off. A reverse mortgage can also use up all of the equity in the home, leaving fewer assets, although most have a clause that prevents the person or the estate from owing more than the value of the home when the loan becomes due and the home is sold (ReverseMorgageproblems.org, 2014).

Federally Sponsored Programs

Federal housing designed specifically for the elderly with services was first established in 1959 under Section 202, Supportive Housing for the Elderly Program of the Department of Housing and Urban Development. The program continues as the primary source of federal housing support for frail older persons. Older renters face the challenge of finding affordable rents. Rising rents often make it impossible for persons to remain in the community. Elders with very low income pay a median of $700 a month on rent and struggle to meet their housing costs. Yet, only 24% of all renters receive federal rental assistance (HUD, 2009).

Section 202, provides capital for the development and expansion of supportive housing for elders with low income, as well as rent subsidies for the residents to help cover the difference between the operating costs of the building and their individual rent. Rents are limited to 20% of the tenant's income. Tenants are primarily elderly women living alone with incomes between $5,000 and $15,000 (HUD, 2008). Renters must usually pay up to 30% of their income toward rent and the program pays the difference.

Section 202 is also intended to ensure that residents have access to services that can assist them to live independently, such as meals, transportation, personal assistance, and housekeeping. Housing managers are expected to be able to assess resident needs, coordinate services, and seek needed assistance. Residents must be at least 62 years of age with an income below 50% of the area median income. HUD provides some funding to projects that can assist them in hiring service coordinators who link tenants with services.

The program is actually a partnership between the older renter, the federal government, and the apartment owner. But the ability of the program to meet the needs of older renters is restricted due to limited funding. Funding for 2012 was $375 million and decreased to $355 million in 2013, with a request for $400 million for FY 2014 (HUD, 2013). Thus, the demand continues to outpace the supply, meaning that many who could continue to live in the community through this supportive housing program may be forced into more restrictive institutional care.

Section 8 Housing

Section 8 provides rental assistance to low-income families, elderly, and disabled persons. A person is eligible if his or her gross income does not exceed 50% of HUD's median income guidelines. The program operates by providing vouchers to public housing authorities, which are to be used for partial payment of the rents of low-income persons. Similar to Section 202 payments, the payments that go directly to the landlords are usually the difference between the local standard payment and 30% of the tenant's income. In contrast to the Section 202 program, where renters can use the funds to rent any private apartment, Section 8, Rental Assistance, is used in specific developments. The main form of assistance is a voucher. The elderly comprise 46% of those in the program (Center on Budget and Policy Priorities, 2013). To be part of the voucher program, the housing authority must show that it is responsive to the housing assistance needs of the tenants. Participants in the program are free to choose any housing that will accept the voucher, and which the housing authority approves.

Without any new legislation, the sequester (automatic budget cuts) of March 2013 is expected to cut the number of low-income persons in Section 8 by 140,000 in 2014 (Rice, 2013). This will occur as housing agencies will receive 6% less funding than in the previous year (Rice, 2013). Consequently, many with vouchers will be placed on waiting lists and others may have their vouchers withdrawn. With possible rent reductions, landlords may also become more tentative about accepting vouchers. Moreover, housing authorities have frozen new Section 8 rental assistance vouchers due to the sequestration that occurred in March 2013. As with Section 202 housing, the need for this program will continue to transcend the actual availability of the units.

Continuing Care Retirement Communities

Continuing care retirement communities (CCRCs) or life care communities integrate independent housing, assisted living, and nursing home care under one setting. Thus, they offer the possibility of adjusting the environment to the needs for assistance of the older person. The communities typically provide personal care, social and recreational services, and congregate meals. The continuum of onsite services related to the changing functional status of the older person means that residents are not at risk of eviction if they become impaired or their impairment worsens. Access to medical and long-term care services is often cited as a reason for moving into the communities (Groger & Kinney, 2006). The communities provide the possibility of living in one location even as needs for assistance increase.

Approximately 60% of CCRCs charge an entrance fee, with the remainder being rentals. Typically, residents may be charged an entrance fee that can range from $20,000 for a rental agreement to $1 million for a purchase depending on the size and location of the community. Monthly fees range from $3,000 to $5,000 or more depending on the contract and service plan. Some communities may require that the applicant have long-term care insurance or the person apply for Medicaid or SSI as protection against exhausting their resources. Such requirements mean that the communities are largely inaccessible to low-income older adults.

Although the CCRCs provide many benefits to residents, including a sense of security with access to services, the facilities also involve specific risks. Financial difficulties can result in raising monthly fees and, if a community fails, residents may lose all or part of their entrance fee. As a result of the 2008 recession, occupancy rates for CCRCs declined from 94% to about 89%, with fewer new facilities (Adler, 2012). Although most residents appear to be satisfied, they can become dissatisfied if policies change, such as unexpected charges for services or a shift in programs (GAO, 2010).

With no federal regulation of CCRCs, contracts and regulations vary among states. Consequently, it is critical that potential residents understand the contracts and the stability of the community. Those contemplating a move to a CCRC must also educate themselves about the services provided and the extent to which the housing will meet their future needs.

Assisted Living

Assisted living as a housing option for those needing some assistance with care has grown in the United States. In 2010 there were 31,000 facilities with 733,400 residents (National Center for Assisted Living 2014). The majority of residents were female, 85 years or older, and needed help with at least one activity of daily living; almost half, 42%, had Alzheimer's disease or another form of dementia. Typically, assisted living offers choices of apartment sizes and types.

Upon admission, a licensed nurse assesses residents to determine the level of care needed and any additional costs that would be required. More than half require assistance with meal preparation, medication management, and bathing. A point system is used to measure the type of assistance needed and its frequency, and this is reflected in the monthly costs. Some facilities use a level of care method with residents paying according to their needs.

In 2012, the national average cost for assisted living was $3,550 per month or $37,752 per year, as compared to $79,935 in a nursing home (MetLife, 2012). Residents can expect a 3% to 5% annual increase in their base rates, with costs varying by geographic location. Medicare does not pay for assisted living while Medicaid may pay for assisted living under the Medicaid Waiver program for home and community services.

In 2010, only 19% of residents received Medicaid funding. States remain anxious about including assisted living as a benefit as it would lead to increased utilization, especially if targeted only to those who would otherwise enter a nursing home. Long-term care insurance may also cover assisted living if the policy covers care in a licensed facility. Veterans' benefits may also cover assisted living, taking into consideration the individual's financial assets.

Assisted living facilities are regulated by states; no federal regulations exist. Most regulations relate to the physical characteristics of the facilities and minimum services. States can decide on resident requirements and whether to accept those who are eligible for the nursing home. Access to units such as apartments also varies as Medicaid often does not cover them.

Particularly troubling are issues related to the absence of regulation or oversight in the assisted living industry. With the majority of homes being for-profit facilities with little regulation, the quality of care that is provided—along with the education, training, and experience of those providing this care—is questionable. Facilities are not permitted to provide medical care, although they may dispense medications through medical technicians. Moreover, most are admitted without a thorough assessment of their status; thus, they may not be appropriate for the level of assistance that is provided. Many of those entering facilities have at least the beginning stages of dementia and their ability to continue to function in assisted living is often questionable.

Key challenges for assisted living are to make it affordable and accessible for more people, and most important, to assure that it provides a living situation that is appropriate to the status and needs of its residents. It provides a setting in the long-term care continuum that can be appropriate to the needs of many older persons, but because of its costs, it often remains unaffordable. At the same time, the quality of the care that it offers is often circumspect as the profit motive linked with the absence of government regulations can severely compromise its services. Without federal regulations and licensures, including the use of routine surveys, the quality of the facilities cannot be assured.

Naturally Occurring Retirement Communities

Naturally occurring retirement communities (NORCs) are apartment houses, complexes, or even neighborhoods in which a majority of the residents are over the age of 65 years. These are not planned communities but ones in which persons have naturally aged. Since 2002, the federal government through the Administration on Aging has appropriated over $25 million for 50 NORCs. Federal funding for the program was provided through the CIAIP of the Administration on Aging, but NORCs have not been included in the federal budget since 2011 (NORCs, 2013).

NORCs provide four main categories of services: case management and social work; health care management and assistance; education, socialization, and recreation; and volunteer opportunities. Programs may also offer transportation, meals and information, and referral. All programs have at least one paid staff person. Programs and services focus on assisting the residents to remain independent in their homes, and are usually provided by public and private partnerships. The services also attempt to identify those most vulnerable and at risk in the communities.

Greenfield, Scharlach, Graham, Davitt, and Lehning (2012) provide a summary of the key features in NORC programs. Most utilize volunteers, but all have at least one paid staff person. In addition, budgets depend on a mix of funding, including government sources, private foundations, and a small contribution from residents. About one-third are housed in apartment buildings and another third in neighborhoods, with most being in urban areas. Most programs also engage in advocacy efforts, such as working for more funding or improvements in the sites.

NORCs, through their focus on the involvement of older persons in the community both as advocates and as service volunteers, are actively fulfilling the human right of persons to participate in the community. Moreover, these involvements increase support networks and contribute to a sense of community and belonging (Guo & Castillo, 2012).

The Village Model

The village model for aging in place builds upon the NORC concept but differs slightly in that it depends upon grassroots organizations that evolve out of the involvement of the residents themselves. These residents pay membership dues while also soliciting funds from donations and sponsorships. Although most villages start as completely volunteer associations, they tend to hire at least one staff person, often a social worker. In 2012, there were 66 villages open with more than 100 in development (Poor, Baldwin, & Willett, 2012). Membership ranges from 100 to 800 people, with an average of 200 people; membership fees range from $430 for an individual to $600 for a household (Scharlach,

Lehning, & Graham, 2010). Many villages have reduced fees for residents who are unable to afford the normal fee.

Villages are self-governing and supporting and they work toward creating partnerships with existing resources to bring services into the community. As with the NORCs, they actively engage volunteers who help persons to access resources. However, in contrast to NORCs they usually do not provide professional services such as health care or social work. They tend to focus on companionship, homemaking assistance, and transportation. Many also have social, cultural, and wellness programs and assist persons in arranging for the required services. Findings on the impact of the villages show that they are greatest in promoting social engagement and service access with residents saying they improve their ability to age in place (Graham, Scharlach, and Wolf, 2014).

As the village model continues to develop, states and local areas are beginning to show interest in their development, and in some areas there is joint programming with senior centers. It permits staff to connect with others and to share expertise and plans. The village model predominantly serves middle- and upper-class older adults with little ethnic diversity (Scharlach, Graham, & Lehning, 2012). However, as they continue to develop and potentially receive increased government funding, they may be able to reach lower income and more diverse older persons who have the same goal: to live independently as long as they can in their own home and in their community.

Transportation

A key factor in the ability to live with liberty and security is having accessible and available transportation. As people age, deterioration in vision and reaction abilities, as well as physical changes, may impact their mobility and thus their ability to access services and participate in the community. Research suggests that by 2015, more than 15.5 million older Americans will have a need for more transportation options (deGood, 2012). The need for transportation is particularly acute in rural areas where the elderly face a high risk of isolation due to long distances to their communities and services.

Transportation plays a major role in enabling older persons to remain in the community. Data from a survey of the use of transportation services by impaired older adults show that most of those using these programs were women living alone and who had several limitations in ADLs (Robinson et al., 2012). The service was primarily utilized for medical services and congregate meals programs that combat social isolation. The users of these transportation services felt that these services were critical in allowing them to remain at home. Many localities offer older adults reduced fares on public transportation.

The major sources of federal funding for specialized transportation for older adults and adults with disabilities come from the Federal Transit Administration (FTA) and the Administration for Community Living (ACL). The FTA funds the Transportation for Elderly Persons and Person with Disabilities Program; this program provides funding to states for assisting private nonprofit groups to meet the transportation needs of these groups. The funding is primarily for capital expenses, such as vans, that are specifically meant to meet the needs of older adults and those with disabilities.

In 2012, the Research and Demonstration Program to Improve Coordinated Transportation for People with Disabilities and Older Adults was established between the ACL and the FTA. This program identifies models and approaches to community transportation focused on designing and implementing coordinated transportation systems that are responsive to the needs of the elderly and disabled (ACL, 2014). An important aspect of the progam is that it engages members of both communities in the development and operation of these transportation systems, an aspect that underscores the right to participation. The federal government provides 80% of the funding, with the local costs being only 20%.

Alternatives to public transportation for older adults and the disabled include three general types. Paratransit services provide door-to-door transportation using small vans at reduced fares or on a donation basis, which usually require advance reservations and also charge small fees. Fixed route systems stop at designated places and do not require reservations, although they also charge fees. Ridesharing programs coordinate travel in automobiles, often driven by volunteers. Agencies may provide transportation to human service programs such as senior centers and day health programs. Some programs also provide escort/assistance that includes staying with the user at his or her destination. Instead of charging fees, programs may also provide users with vouchers that pay for the transportation.

Among the recommendations for transportation improvement are increasing transit funding for programs that support mobility options, having localities fund transportation through taxes, increasing federal support of specialized transportation, increased incentives for volunteers who assist with driving, and greater coordination of specialized transportation at the local level (Lynott, Fox-Grage, & Guzman, 2013; National Association of Area Agencies on Aging, 2012). In addition, the mobility of older adults may also be facilitated by environmental adjustments such as improving access to subway systems, instituting unlimited bus stops, increasing bus routes, and providing more and affordable door-to-door transportation.

SUMMARY

The rights to life, liberty, and security of person remain threatened for many older adults, particularly for those without adequate resources to pay for them. The CIAIP, which briefly existed for three years, is evidence of the federal government's recognition of the service needs of older adults in the community if they are to maintain their independence. Although funding has ended, the findings from the funded programs may provide models that can be implemented in other areas with local monies.

Appropriate, affordable, and accessible housing for older adults is critical if they are to remain in the community. Unfortunately, funding for such housing remains restricted, with needs far exceeding the supply. The right to remain independent and secure as long as possible remains compromised due to the absence of sufficient affordable housing. The costs of programs such as continuing care, assisted living, and the village model remain too expensive for the majority of older Americans and federal assistance through subsidies is very limited (Assisted Living Federation of America, 2014).

Assistive technology that can offer security to many in their homes is being rapidly developed but is generally not covered by any public program except for limited coverage through Medicare and Medicaid. Consequently, people must pay privately for the devices that again are unaffordable for many older adults.

Transportation is a critical service necessary for many older adults to remain in the community. Efforts are being made to develop appropriate accessible transportation for older adults and those with disabilities. It is particularly important to note that the Research and Development Program is involving these groups in all phases of the program, a positive affirmation of their human right to participate in the community.

Guardianship, which is designed to protect security and independence of the most vulnerable older adults, continues to be a program that may, in fact, threaten these rights. An absence of federal regulations, insufficient monitoring, lack of trained personnel, and the absence of comprehensive and common assessments are issues that must be considered if the quality of the programs is to improve. Without such changes, the rights of the most vulnerable continue to be placed at risk by the program intended to defend them.

Finally, there is an awareness and understanding of the issues confronting older adults that impact their ability to remain independent in the community. Efforts are being made to deal with these issues, although resources remain limited. Assuring adequate funding that can promote their accessibility and effectiveness is necessary if they are to be available to all older adults so that both their needs and rights to remain in their homes and community can be met.

QUESTIONS FOR DISCUSSION

1. Discuss how guardianship impacts the rights of older adults. What are some of the major concerns with the program?

2. What is meant by aging in place? What is required to enable it to occur? How does it relate to human rights?

3. What are some of the weaknesses of assisted living?

4. Thinking about yourself, where do you think you would like to live as an older adult? What type of housing, community, and so on appeal to you? Be as specific as possible.

REFERENCES

AARP Public Policy Institute. (2005). *Livable communities: An evaluation guide.* Washington, DC: Author.

AARP Public Policy Institute. (2011). *Housing for older adults: The impacts of the recession.* Washington, DC: Author.

Adler, J. (2012). *Bankruptcy woes continue for CCRCs, National Real Estate Investor, January.* Retrieved from http://nreionline.com/seniors-housing/bankruptcy-woes-continue-ccrcs

Alley, D., Liebig, P., Pynoos, J., Banerjee, T., & Choi, I. H. (2007). Creating elder-friendly communities: Preparations for an aging society. *Journal of Gerontological Social Work, 49*(1/2), 1–18.

Assisted Living Federation of America. (2014). *Cost of assisted living.* Retrieved from http://www.alfa.org/alfa/Assessing_Cost.asp

Center on Budget and Policy Priorities. (2013). *Policy basics: Section 8 project-based rental assistance.* Washington, DC: Author.

Center for Elders and Courts. (2014). *Guardianship basic.* Retrieved from http://www.eldersandcourts.org

Center for Housing Policy. (2012). *Housing an aging population: Are we prepared?* Washington, DC: Author.

Commerce Department. (2008). *American housing survey for the United States, 2007.* Washington, DC: Author.

Community Innovations for Aging in Place (CIAIP) Final Report. (2014). Retrieved from http://www.ciaip.org/docs/final_grantee_report.pdf

deGood, K. (2012). *Aging in place, stuck without options.* Washington, DC: Transportation for America.

Freedman, V., & Agree, E. (2008). *Home modifications: Use, costs, and interaction with functioning among-near elderly and older adults.* Retrieved from http://aspe.hhs.gov/daltcp/reports/2008/homemod.pdf

GAO. (2010). *Older Americans: Continuing care retirement communities can provide benefits but not without some risk.* Washington, DC: Government Printing Office.

Graham, C., Scharlach, A., Wolf, J. (2014). The impact of the village model onhealth,well-being, service access and social engagement of older adults, *Health, Education and Behavior, 41*, 945–975.

Greenfield, E., Scharlach, A., Graham, C., Davitt, J., & Lehning, A. (2012). *An overview of programs in the National NORCs Aging in Place Initiative: Results from a 2012 organizational survey.* New Brunswick: Rutgers University School of Social Work.

Groger, L., & Kinney, J. (2006). CCRC here we come: Reasons for moving to a continuing care retirement community. *Journal of Housing for the Elderly, 20*, 79–101.

Guo, K., & Castillo, R. (2012). The U.S. long term care system: Development and expansion of naturally occurring retirement communities as an innovative model for aging in place. *Ageing International, 37*, 210–227.

Koppen, J. (2009). *Effect of the economy on housing choices.* AARP Knowledge Management. Washington, DC: AARP.

Lawton, M. (1980). *Environment and aging.* Monterey: Brooks/Cole.

Liu, S., & Lapane, K. (2009). Residential modifications and decline in physical function among community-dwelling older adults. *The Gerontologist, 39*, 344–354.

Lynott, J., Fox-Grage, W., & Guzman, S. (2013). *Weaving it together: A tapestry of transportation funding for older adults.* AARP, Public Policy Institute. Washington, DC: Author.

MetLife. (2012). *Market survey of long-term care costs.* Retrieved from https://www.metlife.com/mmi/research/2012-market-survey-long-term-care-costs.html#keyfindings

Moye, J., & Naik, A. (2011). Preserving rights for individuals facing guardianship. *Journal of the American Medical Association, 305*, 936–937.

National Association of Area Agencies on Aging. (2012). *Policy priorities that promote the health, security & well-being of older adults.* Washington, DC: Author.

National Association of Home Builders. (2011). *Funding for home modifications and programs.* Washington, DC: Author.

National Center for Assisted Living. (2014). *Assisted living community profile.* Retrieved from http://www.ahcancal.org/ncal/resources/pages/alfacilityprofile.aspx

NORCs. (2013). *Community innovations for Aging in Place Program.* Retrieved from http://www.norcs.org/page.aspx?id=196818

Poor, S., Baldwin, C., & Willett, J. (2012). The village movement empowers older adults to stay connected to home and community. *Generations, 36*, 112–117.

Reverse Mortgage Problems.org. (2014). *The basics of reverse mortgage problems.* Retrieved from http://www.reversemortgageproblems.org

Rice, D. (2013). *Sequestration could deny rental assistance to 140,000 low-income families.* Washington, DC: Center on Budget and Policy Priorities.

Scharlach, A., Graham, C., & Lehning, A. (2012). The village model: A consumer-driven approach for aging in place. *The Gerontologist, 52,* 418–427.

Scharlach, A., Lehning, A., & Graham, C. (2010). *A demographic profile of village members.* Berkeley, University of California Berkeley: Center for Advanced Study of Aging Services.

United Nations. (2002). *Madrid International Plan of Action on Ageing.* 8–12 April. Madrid: Author.

U.S. Department of Housing and Urban Development. (2008). *Section 202 Supportive Housing for the Elderly: Program status and performance measurement.* Washington, DC: Author. Retrieved from http://www.aarp.org/content/dam/aarp/research/public_policy_institute/liv_com/2012/rural-transportation-AARP-ppi-liv-com.pdf

U.S. Department of Housing and Urban Development. (2009). *Report to Congress: Worst case housing needs.* Washington, DC: Author. Retrieved from http://portal.hud.gov/hudportal/documents/huddoc?id=Housing_Elderly_2012.pdf

U.S. Department of Housing and Urban Development. (2013). *The federal budget and its impact on National Housing Programs.* Washington, DC: Author.

U.S. Department of Housing and Urban Development. (2014). *Section 202 Supportive Housing Program for the Elderly.* Washington, DC: Author. Retrieved from http://web20.nixonpeabody.com/ahrc/Assets/Section%20202%20Briefing_FY%202014.pdf

Wagner, S., Shubair, M., & Michalos, A. (2010). Surveying older adults' options on housing: Recommendations for policy. *Social Indicators Research, 99,* 405–412.

Wahl, H., Fange, A., Oswald, F., Gitlin, L., & Iwarson, S. (2009). The home environment and disability-related outcomes in aging individuals: What is the empirical evidence? *The Gerontologist, 49,* 355–367.

Wood, E., & O'Bryan, M. (2012). Assessment of civil capacities: An evaluative framework and practical recommendations. In G. Demakis (Ed.), *Civil capacities in clinical neuropsychology: Research findings and recommendations* (pp. 185–205). New York, NY: Oxford University Press.

CHAPTER 5

Policy and the Right to Health and Health Care

The rights to health and health care in the event of illness, disability, or old age are detailed in Article 25 of the Universal Declaration of Human Rights (UNDHR). These rights are fundamental to the well-being of older adults as their needs for medical care increase with age. As episodes of acute illness decline, chronic conditions increase with age, impacting both individuals and society. Chronic conditions such as arthritis and heart disease permeate many areas of a person's life, often increasing demands for an array of support. These conditions also have a large impact on the health care system; in fact, they comprise approximately 75% of the total U.S. health care expenditures (National Health Council, 2014).

CHRONIC ILLNESS AND LONG-TERM CARE

The illnesses affecting older adults differ from those of younger persons, in that they tend to be chronic rather than acute. As illnesses progress, both physical and mental functioning can decline, and the need for assistance increases. This assistance comprises long-term services and support (LTSS), which includes all of the support that a person may need to help him or her with functioning (Congressional Business Office [CBO], 2014). The majority of such assistance is provided in the community, primarily informally by family and friends (CBO, 2014).

Since the Supreme Court Olmstead Decision of 1999, states are required to provide assistance to those with limitations in the least restrictive environment in accordance with their needs. This resulted in states shifting from a focus on institutional care, such as nursing homes, to more home- and community-based services. Thus, Medicaid funding for long-term care shifted from 80% going to institutional care and 20% to community care in 1995 to 55% and 40%, respectively, in 2011 (Kaiser Family Foundation, 2014a).

However, even with this focus, accessing community services can be difficult. LTSS are fragmented, provided by a variety of sources with many gaps between them. Navigating the long-term care maze is in itself a taxing ordeal that can overwhelm and frustrate many persons seeking support. Caregivers can easily become frustrated and feel further isolated while attempting to locate specific services and funding sources. In fact, the effort to find such assistance can place an extra burden on them (Miller, Allen, & Mor, 2009).

Long-term care is costly and quickly exhausts the resources of most persons. Nationally, nursing home rates average a total of $212 a day, while the median cost of a homemaker or home health aid is $19 and $20 an hour (Genworth, 2014). Individuals pay for the care through their personal resources and, on reaching the financial eligibility criteria, turn to Medicaid. Few Americans actually plan for any future long-term care needs and, consequently, do not have the income or assets to pay for it.

Long-term care insurance designed to assist persons in paying for services remains expensive and unaffordable for most people. Moreover, since 2010, many insurers have stopped selling policies, resulting in only 7 million people maintaining insurance. At the same time, benefits continue to be cut while premiums increase (Gage, Tobin, & Sanghavi, 2013). Under the Affordable Care Act (ACA) of 2010, people were permitted to buy coverage for $5 per month, which would provide them with $18,000 of benefits per year when needed, but the program ended in 2011. Subsequently, a federal Commission on Long-Term Care was established to help find solutions to long-term care concerns. Unfortunately, the Committee's report, released in September 2013, showed no consensus on how to finance the system (Commission on Long-Term Care, 2013).

Along with financing, a persistent concern in the LTSS is the availability of trained and skilled persons to provide the services. Data from the Commission's report testify to the shortage of board-certified geriatricians, geriatric psychiatrists, and geriatric social workers. In addition, nurse's aides and nursing assistants who provide the bulk of care in nursing homes have high turnover rates; therefore, facilities have difficulties attracting and retaining them. Poor pay, low benefits, and limited career opportunities contribute to a shortage of workers. In addition, the commission also questioned whether the 75 hours minimum training requirement imposed by the federal government for nursing assistants and home health aides working in Medicare-certified programs is sufficient to meet the complex needs of the older adults in their care.

MEDICARE

Medicare was developed in the 1960s to address the needs of the aging population with regard to health care. However, there is a growing concern as to whether the program can meet the needs of today's aging population. Findings from one study indicate that those with multiple disabilities are among those most likely to delay seeing a physician, even with Medicare coverage (Lee, Hasnain-Wynia, & Lau, 2011). Co-pays, restricted benefits for home and community services (including home care), and limited payments for hospital and nursing home care are among the factors that limit its relevance to the long-term care needs of older adults.

Medicare Part A is hospital insurance that for most people is paid for through payroll taxes. It covers in-patient hospital care and some short-term skilled nursing stays, as well as hospice care and limited home health care. Under Part A, recipients have an annual deductible for 1–60 days ($1,184 in 2013) of in-patient care and then must pay coinsurance for days 61–90 ($592 in 2013). After day 91, they are in the 60 lifetime reserve days with payments of $592 per day. Once the lifetime reserve is reached, the beneficiary is responsible for all costs.

Medicare Part B is medical insurance for which people pay a monthly premium that covers physician services and some outpatient care, such as physical and occupational therapy and some home health care. It may also cover medical supplies. Part C (Medicare Advantage) comprises private health care plans.

Medicare Part C (Medicare Advantage) combines hospital care (Part A) with outpatient care (Part B) by offering care through a health maintenance organization (HMO) or a preferred provider plan (PPO). The plans are offered through private insurance companies that are approved by Medicare and may lower costs for services. However, the beneficiary must get all care through the plan. Plans vary with regard to benefits and premiums, with most offering prescription drug coverage.

Medicare Part D is prescription drug coverage that is offered through specific drug plans. Persons select the plan that best fits their needs and pay a monthly premium that is related to their income as well as a monthly plan premium. Persons with income below 150% of the poverty level are eligible for subsidies that help with premiums, deductibles, and co-payments. Plans vary in terms of deductibles and the amount of co-payment that is required. A coverage gap, "doughnut hole," occurs when the enrollee has paid drug costs of $2,970 and remains until drug expenses reach $4,750. At that level, catastrophic coverage begins with the beneficiary again being covered by paying a maximum of 5% of the costs of each drug. The ACA will begin closing the doughnut hole by decreasing the share of drug costs that beneficiaries must pay until it reaches 25% in 2020 (Medicare.gov, 2014a).

Medicare's solvency is a major concern. There is expected to be an unfunded liability of $43 trillion in Medicare over the next 75 years as the Trust Fund will not be able to meet its expenditures (Medicare Trustees, 2013). Without program reforms, it is expected that by 2024, the program will not be able to meet its financial obligations to a rapidly aging population.

Medicare and Human Rights

The Medicare program, although focused on older adults, was not designed to cover their long-term care needs. Consequently, its effectiveness in meeting the needs and rights of many older adults is limited through its many program restrictions that are not commensurate with the demands of their chronic conditions.

The right to health care under Medicare is also challenged through access to the system itself. Navigating the system of benefits and comprehending its procedures and regulations can be difficult for many older adults. Moreover, understanding the nuances of the program and its many parts can act as a barrier to effective utilization of services. Understanding supplemental coverage that can help reduce costs is particularly difficult for those with lower cognitive ability or those who have difficulty comprehending numbers, making them vulnerable to not receiving the financial protections available to others (Chan & Elbel, 2012).

MEDICAID

Medicaid, Title XIX, under the Social Security Act was passed in 1965 to provide health care for those below the poverty line. Under the program, participating states are required to provide care for pregnant women, children, older adult Medicare recipients, adults under 65 years with dependent children, children, and adults with disabilities. Nursing home care must be covered, but other long-term care services are optional. As a federal-state program, each state is permitted to develop its own eligibility criteria, poverty guidelines, and remuneration schedules. In addition, states are responsible for contributing up to half of the funding for their programs. States are also permitted to expand services under the ACA.

In contrast to Medicare, Medicaid is not an insurance program, as recipients have not paid directly into it. Rather, it is a means-tested needs-based program with eligibility based primarily on income and assets. The ACA permits states to expand Medicaid coverage by raising the eligibility criteria to incomes up to 133% of the poverty line. Some recipients are considered dual-eligible, in that they receive Medicare as well as Medicaid. Individuals must also meet federal and state immigration and residency requirements.

Medicaid is the principal provider of all long-term health care in the United States. It covers nearly 60% of all nursing home residents and 62% of all LTSS Services (Commission on Long-Term Care, 2013). Total spending on long-term care rose from $113 billion in 2007 to nearly $140 billion in 2012 (AARP, 2014). According to AARP, nearly one-third of all seniors will exhaust their resources and have to turn to Medicaid for long-term care as the costs of LTSS continue to be unaffordable for middle-income families.

Under the Medicaid program, states are permitted through the Home and Community-Based Waiver (HCBS) Program to provide long-term care services in the home and community rather than in an institution. Services must be targeted to those needing nursing homes. The possible services are much broader than those provided through Medicare and include case management, homemaker, home health aide, personal care, adult day health services, rehabilitation, transportation, and respite care. Waivers are expected to be budget neutral, in that the cost of services must not exceed the cost of care in a nursing facility. But, as Medicaid continues to take more of a state's budget, states have begun to enact measures of cost containment with regard to waivers (Kaiser Family Foundation, 2014b). In order to control costs, states used more restrictive financial eligibility criteria, stricter functional eligibility, and caps on services in comparison to nursing home eligibility.

In addition to HCBS, Medicaid waivers also permit states to offer personal care services (PCS) that can help persons to remain independent in their homes. These include assistance with housework and meal preparation. States decide what services to offer, but they usually involve assistance with activities of daily living. A recent evaluation of the program found problems with state compliance, payments, and fraud, with states having inadequate controls on the services, including the quality of the home attendants (U.S. Department of Health and Human Services [DHHS], 2012).

However, even with these programs, the bulk of Medicaid money (70%) is spent on nursing homes (Centers for Medicare and Medicaid Services [CMS], 2013). At the same time, there remains a serious unmet need for HCBS, as underscored by data from 2010 that show 120,000 elderly and disabled persons on waiting lists for services for an average of 10 months (Ng, Harrington, & Kitchener, 2010).

MEDICAID AND HUMAN RIGHTS

Medicaid remains an expensive program, with the federal and state government spending over $400 billion on the program in 2010, and it is expected to grow 7% per year (DHHS, 2012). In order to prevent the program from collapsing, proposals have been suggested to cut costs; these include shifting to a block grant proposal through which the federal government would allot each state an annual lump sum payment for the program with the amount being less than matching funds; a managed care model for long-term care, with states paying private insurance companies a fixed amount of money per Medicaid long-term care recipient and the company deciding on the services; and limiting the number of people eligible for benefits by extending the period of time when assets can be transferred beyond the present 5-year acceptable period.

Each of these proposals impacts the human rights of older persons. The block grant proposal could compromise the quality of health care as states would attempt to hold down costs, which could mean many doing without the needed services. As states are permitted to change eligibility rules, they may also curtail the assets and income that a community-dwelling spouse of a nursing home resident is able to maintain, severely undermining their ability to remain financially secure. Under the managed care model, programs may limit services in order to save money and to assure profits that could undermine the efficacy of services in meeting the health care needs of recipients. The lengthened transfer of assets period would limit the number of persons eligible for Medicaid and thus cause further hardship and burden to those unable to pay health care costs. Most important, many would be denied access to care.

PROGRAM OF ALL-INCLUSIVE CARE FOR THE ELDERLY

Program of All-Inclusive Care for the Elderly (PACE) provides all Medicare and Medicaid services to persons 55 years and older living in the community. It is focused on those who would otherwise need nursing home care but who, with assistance from PACE, can remain in the community. The program is paid for by Medicare and Medicaid funds.

Participants must also live in a PACE-served community. It thus aims to meet older adults' rights to protection, security, and independence.

In addition to the traditional services provided through Medicare and Medicaid, it also covers prescription drugs, transportation, home care, hospital visits, and even some nursing home stays. An interdisciplinary team of professionals cares for each participant. As prescription medications are covered, persons do not need a separate Part D Drug Plan. The programs also provide support to caregivers through training and support groups as well as respite care. As of 2014, 104 PACE programs were operational in 31 states (National PACE Association, 2014). Participants usually attend adult day care several times a month; if 24-hour day care is needed, PACE will cover it either in an assisted living facility or in a nursing home.

PACE has been found to have higher quality of care and better outcomes for its clients than other settings (Edmondson, 2012). However, programs remain limited in scale due to barriers that limit their flexibility and ability to provide quality care. Payment issues include variations in Medicaid payments among the states, the unpredictability of federal and state capitation payments, and a lack of program standardization across states that cause variation in the ways in which regulations are interpreted (Hansen & Hewitt, 2012). However, striving to help older adults to live securely in the community with health care services and supports reflects key human rights values.

HOME HEALTH CARE

Many older persons could remain in their homes if they had some assistance. However, Medicare typically covers home health care for 60 days and only if the person is housebound and requires a certain level of skilled care. It does not pay for personal or homemaker services. Medicaid assistance varies by state but is typically 2 to 8 hours a day, with the total costs of care not exceeding the cost of care in a nursing home. The provided services can include both personal and homemaker assistance such as cooking, cleaning, and laundry. Recently, the personal care services under Medicaid have been questioned with regard to fraud and improper payments, with recommendations given for assuring the quality and integrity of the program so that it may continue to serve vulnerable persons (DHHS, 2012).

The majority of home care is paid for directly by the recipient and can average $21,000 per year for a part-time worker, with the average hourly rate for home health aides provided by a home care agency at $19 per hour (www.maturemarketinstitute.com). These costs mean that those not eligible for Medicaid and without the finances to cover the expense are often without access to the service. Access is further compromised by a 2011 requirement that mandates Medicare beneficiaries see a doctor 90 days before beginning services or 30 days after in order for the agency to be reimbursed. Requiring these visits could place an untold burden on homebound and rural elderly who have difficulty getting to a physician (Kaiser Health News, 2011).

CONSUMER-DIRECTED CARE PROGRAMS

Consumer-directed care programs have the older person responsible for hiring the care provider and determining the services he or she wants. There are basically two models. In the first model, the employer has the authority to hire, manage, and fire workers without going through a home care agency. The second model gives budget authority to the participant with the ability to pay for home care or use the money to purchase goods and services that can assist him or her to function.

Medicaid programs in some states permit participants to pay relatives, including spouses, for care. For many, this has reduced the stress of caregiving and in some cases has permitted caregivers to spend more time providing assistance. In addition, some long-term care insurance policies also permit beneficiaries to pay family members for care.

The idea of consumer-directed care continues to expand. Under the ACA, a new Medicaid option under the waiver plans, Community First Choice (CFC), gives participants the authority to employ spouses or other relatives to provide care. Money can also be used to purchase other goods or supports that can increase their independence.

Data from 2011 show that there were 298 consumer-directed programs in the United States (Doty et al., 2012). An evaluation of the outcomes of programs in three states showed that participants had better access to paid services and fewer unmet needs for assistance, with increased satisfaction with the quality of services and their quality of life in comparison to a control group (Benjamin & Fennell, 2007). By increasing control, they enhance feelings of empowerment and the right to participation.

However, the programs can be stressful for consumers with dementia, as well as their families (Tilly, 2007). Consequently, Tilly's report on consumer-directed programs included recommendations that programs should be an option for these participants but that states must use careful assessments to assure that the person can manage services; have specialized professionals who can help participants, if needed; and ensure quality of care through monitoring and frequent contacts.

MENTAL HEALTH

The demand for mental health care for older adults can be expected to expand while policies remain fragmented and providers remain scarce. The extent of the need for services is underscored by estimates that 20.4% of adults 65 years and over meet the criteria for having a mental disorder, including dementia, in the previous 12 months (Karel, Gatz, & Smyer, 2012). Predictions are that the number of older adults with mental disorders will increase to 15 million in 2030 and that an increasing number of these persons will be seeking mental health services.

Access to mental health care remains a problem for older adults who are less likely than younger persons to receive services and are less likely to receive services from a mental health specialist (Bogner et al., 2009). Instead, they are prone to receiving treatment from a primary care practitioner who does not necessarily have any training in geriatric mental health. This practitioner is easier to access; in addition, primary care does not hold the stigma that may be associated with using mental health services (Conner et al., 2010).

Mental health care for older adults comprises many systems including those for acute and chronic mental health, long-term care, medical health, dementia care, and rehabilitation systems (Knight & Sayegh, 2011). Most services are funded through Medicare and Medicaid, although they are also offered by a variety of programs, both for profit and nonprofit programs. The trend has consistently been to shift the provision of mental health care to the states; thus, services and programs vary. However, the overall outcome has been that older adults with clinical mental health disorders are less likely than others to receive specialized mental health services (Kaskie, Gregory, & Cavanaugh, 2008). In addition, low rates for Medicaid reimbursement acts as a further barrier to care, as it is often difficult to find a provider who accepts Medicaid payments.

Since the Mental Health Parity and Addiction Equity Act of 2001, Medicare began covering expenses at 60% and is expected to achieve parity of 80% in 2014. However, there remains much variability with regard to mental health coverage for services under Medicare as decisions are made by private insurers that administer the Medicare system (Kaskie, Imhof, & Wyatt, 2008). Moreover, as Medicare and Medicaid determine which providers can offer reimbursed mental health care, access for many may be further restricted.

The provision of good mental health services depends in large part upon having a workforce that is trained in geriatric care. The shortage of such specialists is a major gap in the provision of services. The mental health workforce for older adults has been described as insufficient in numbers and diversity and lacking basic competence and knowledge (Institute of Medicine [IOM], 2012). Without skilled practitioners trained in geriatric care, who are able to assess, diagnose, and treat the problems presented by older patients, the quality of the care that they receive will remain questionable.

Dementia

Dementia refers to the loss of mental functions in two or more areas (such as language, memory, visual and spatial abilities, and judgment), to the extent that the loss interferes with normal functioning. Although there are many types of dementia, Alzheimer's disease (AD) is the most common in older adults. In 2010, there were 4.7 million people aged 65 and older with AD dementia in the United States and it is expected that this number will increase dramatically in the next 40 years (Hebert, Weuve, Scherr, & Evans, 2013). The disease has assumed the magnitude of a public health problem as its impact is felt throughout society. Estimates are that care for persons with AD was approximately $220 billion in 2013, including $150 billion paid by Medicare and Medicaid (Alzheimer's Association, 2014).

In January 2011, the National Alzheimer's Project Act (NAPA) was signed into law. The Act is a comprehensive policy that focuses on dealing with the illness through a national plan, coordinated research across federal agencies, accelerated development of treatments, improved early diagnoses and treatment, improved outcomes for ethnic and minority populations, and better coordination among international groups. The plan recognizes the impact that the illness has on individuals, families, and society as a whole. In 2013, the National Institutes of Health (NIH) allocated an additional $40 million in funding for research on therapies that may both prevent and treat the disease. The plan is to be updated annually and thus will offer a framework for research, care, and services.

The Alzheimer's Accountability Act of 2013 (H.R. 4351), which was introduced into Congress in 2014, has set priorities for funding and the needed resources for Alzheimer's research. The NIH, in accordance with the goals of the National Alzheimer's Plan, would establish these priorities. To date, this Act remains in Committee in the House.

The human rights of persons with Alzheimer's disease and related disorders (ADRD) are continually threatened. Their dignity, right to participation, independence, and protection are often overlooked. Access to information and services can be difficult to obtain, which presents an immediate barrier to their care and support. Their rights to security and dignity, as well as the ability to live without violence or abuse, remain in jeopardy along with their right to health care.

NURSING HOMES

More than 1.4 million persons resided in nursing homes in 2011, which equaled 2.9% of the 65 years-plus population and 10.7% of the over 85 years population (CMS, 2012). The majority of residents are women

(67.2%) and non-Hispanic Whites (78.9%), with at least some physical functioning and cognitive impairment. Severe physical or cognitive impairment was present in approximately 16%, and more than one-third were severely incontinent (CMS, 2012). The overall assumption behind nursing homes is that the institution is the best place to receive the needed personal care (Kane, 2010).

Among the key factors leading to nursing home placement are the absence of an informal caregiver and stress among existing caregivers. Such stress is often associated with physical strain, financial hardship, incontinence, and behavior problems (Spillman & Long, 2007). Consequently, interventions that could reduce such stress may deter nursing home entry. But, whatever the reason that leads to admission, nursing homes prevent many from realizing their rights for autonomy and participation in society.

The rights of nursing home residents and the responsibilities of the institutions are outlined in the 1987 Omnibus Budget Reconciliation Act (OBRA'87), which applies to all Medicare and Medicaid certified sites. The rights identified range from that of participating in advocacy groups to being fully informed regarding care and treatment and the right to a resident's privacy and ability to select his or her own doctor. Many of the rights reinforce human rights while also regulating quality care.

All residents, regardless of the form of their payment, are required to receive the same services. However, those on Medicaid are likely to receive less attention than others (Pritchard, 2013). Residents covered by Medicaid are also more at risk than private-pay residents of having their beds released if they have to enter a hospital (Pritchard, 2013). Although the nursing home is required to provide a place for this resident, they may have to stay in the hospital or transfer to another facility before returning.

Nursing homes are required to assess a resident's condition within 14 days of admission and develop a care plan that must be updated quarterly. The resident and the family have a right to participate in the planning process. Residents have the right to be free from any physical or chemical restraints that are not necessary for treating medical symptoms. Consequently, homes cannot use restraints as a means for dealing with problematic and difficult behaviors. Feeding tubes may only be used if medically necessary, and the resident or family can stop the treatment at any time.

The CMS set minimum quality and safety standards that homes must meet in order to receive funding. Over 90% of homes participate in these federal programs and thus must adhere to the 175 standards. States are responsible for monitoring homes for compliance and issuing sanctions if they are not met. Homes must be assessed every 9–15 months. States are also required to investigate any serious complaints and conduct more investigations if they feel they are necessary. There are also federal standards for the number of nurses, nurse's aides, and social workers that a home must have. Nursing home report cards that can help in selecting a facility are available online for the public to review (Medicare.gov, 2014b).

Cultural Change

In the 1990s a cultural change occurred within nursing homes, which aimed to make them less institutional and more resident-centered and homelike. The Eden Alternative model (Thomas, 1996) served as a catalyst for these changes, with its principles for individualized care and resident autonomy, human rights principles, and increasing the quality of life of both residents and staff. Each of its ten principles is related to human growth and fulfillment, with a focus on eliminating loneliness, helplessness, and boredom and having resident-centered care. With regard to resident-centered care, it is noteworthy that staff and residents are referred to as care partners.

Research on the effectiveness and outcomes of the model indicate that it improves both occupancy and revenue for the homes (Elliott, 2010) with potential psychosocial benefits for residents, although the impact on residents' health is inconsistent (Hill, Kolanowski, Milone-Nuzzo, & Yevchak, 2011).

The need for culture change in nursing homes was formally recognized in 2009 when the CMS revised its nursing home guidelines to relate to person-centered care and preferences. Two of the guidelines, dignity and self-determination, and participation, reflect a human rights perspective.

The federal government is also working toward the improvement of quality of nursing homes that also uphold human rights principles. The Action Plan for Further Improvement of Nursing Home Quality (CMS, 2012) was formulated with improving individual care by assuring respect for the dignity of residents and their rights to self-determination. However, enforcing these measures requires regulations and training with guidelines for surveyors to assure that they are actually instituted.

SUMMARY

As long as health care is a commodity, it is difficult to also be a right. Access to health and health care remains dependent upon meeting certain criteria and in most instances is related to financial resources. This selective rather than overall comprehensive nature of the health policies places many older adults at risk of not having their needs or rights met.

Although Medicare focuses on the health care of older adults and Medicaid provides many of the services that they need, each has barriers that impede its effectiveness in addressing this right. The limitations of Medicare with regard to care for the chronic illnesses that impact the functioning of older adults severely limits its role in helping them to attain the highest standard of possible health. Problems of access to the system, whether due to problems in obtaining information or difficulties meeting co-payments, mean that many continue to struggle to obtain services. Its restriction on home-based services that could enable many to remain in the community further impacts their rights to security, protection, and dignity.

Medicaid eligibility criteria restrict its comprehensive services to those with low incomes and those meeting certain immigration requirements. But rather than a universal program, it is selective, consequently denying access to many who could benefit from services. Moreover, as states wrestle with budgets and begin to shrink services, the ability of the programs to provide services remains uncertain.

Both PACE and consumer-directed programs reflect an emphasis on the rights of older adults as each fosters their involvement and participation. Expanding the types of services that also enable people to remain in their communities may further contribute to their independence and well-being while addressing their needs for health care.

Providing for the mental health care of older adults remains a key challenge due to continued access issues and a paucity of skilled practitioners. Moreover, the human rights of those with dementia are particularly vulnerable, with their security and dignity at risk. Although consumer-directed care might empower many cognitively impaired older adults, safeguards to assure their quality of life under the system are essential.

The changes that are occurring within many nursing homes suggest that these institutions are beginning to more fully adopt human rights principles. By becoming more resident-centered, they can assist residents to enjoy their basic human rights to the highest attainable standard of physical and mental health.

QUESTIONS FOR DISCUSSION

1. What is meant by long-term care and how does it relate to older adults?
2. Discuss some of the weaknesses of Medicare with regard to meeting the health care needs of older adults.
3. What factors impact the human rights of older adults needing mental health care or those with dementia?
4. What factors would you emphasize in designing a nursing home to make it reflective of human rights? What types of programs might you have to assure human rights of residents?

REFERENCES

AARP. (2014). *Raising expectations: A state scorecard on long-term services and supports for older adults, people with physical disabilities and family caregivers.* Retrieved from http://www.longtermscorecard.org/~/link.aspx?_id=DCD2C261D26D414C971D574D577A78FE&_z=z#.U7rG7KhQaBR

Alzheimer's Association. (2014). *Disease facts and figures.* Retrieved from http://www.alz.org/alzheimers_disease_facts_and_figures.asp

Benjamin, A. E., & Fennell, M. L. (2007). *Putting consumers first in long-term care: Findings from the cash & counseling demonstration and evaluation.* Hoboken, NJ: Wiley Blackwell.

Bogner, H., de Vries, H., Maulik, P., Unutzer, J. (2009). Mental health services use: Baltimore epidemiologic catchment area follow-up., *The American Journal of Geriatric Psychiatry, 17,* 706–715.

Centers for Medicare and Medicaid Services. (2014). *Medicaid expenditures for long term services and supports,* 2011. Retrieved from http://www.medicaid. gov/medicaid-chip-program-information/by-topics/long-term-services-and-supports/downloads/ltss-expenditure-narr-2011.pdf

Centers for Medicare and Medicaid Services. (2012). *Nursing home data compendium, 2012 Edition.* Washington, DC: Author.

Chan, S., & Elbel, B. (2012). Low cognitive ability and poor skill with numbers may prevent many from enrolling in Medicare supplemental coverage. *Health Affairs, 31,* 1847–1854.

Commission on Long-Term Care. (2013). *Report to Congress.* Retrieved from http://www.medicareadvocacy.org/wp-content/uploads/2014/01/ Commission-on-Long-Term-Care-Final-Report-9-18-13-00042470.pdf

Congressional Budget Office. (2014). *Rising demand for long-term care services and supports for elderly people.* Retrieved from http://www.cbo.gov/ publication/44363

Conner, K., Copeland, V., Grote, N., Koeske, G., Rosen, D., Reynolds, C. (2010). Mental health treatment seeking among older adults with depression: The impact of stigma and race. *American Journal of Geriatric Psychiatry, 18,* 531–543.

Department of Health and Human Services. (2012). Actuarial Report on the financial outlook for Medicaid, Centers for Medicare and Medicaid Services. Washington, DC: Author.

Doty, P., Mahoney, K., Simon-Rusinowitz, L., Sciegah, M., Selkow, I., & Loughlin, D. (2012). How does cash and counseling affect the growth of participant-directed services. *Generations, 36,* 28–36.

Edmondson, R. (2012). PACE is a success. *Modern Healthcare, 42,* 15.

Elliott, E. (2010). Occupancy and revenue gains from culture change in nursing homes: A win-win innovation for a new age of long-term care. *Seniors Housing & Care Journal, 18,* 21–36.

Gage, B., Tobin, J., & Sanghavi, D. (2013). *Disabled Americans facing ruinous costs of long-term care get no new answers from a blue-ribbon federal commission last week. Where do we go from here.* Retrieved from http://www.brookings.edu/ blogs/up-front/posts/2013/09/25-disabled-americans-long-term-care-gage-tobin-sanghavi

Genworth. (2014). Cost of care survey. https://www.genworth.com/dam/Americas/US/PDFs/Consumer/corporate/130568_032514_CostofCare_FINAL_nonsecure.pdf

Hansen, J. & Hewitt, M. (2012). PACE provides a sense of belonging for elders. *Generations, 36*, 37–43.

Hebert, L., Weuve, J., Scherr, P., & Evans, D. (2013). Alzheimer disease in the United States (2010–2050). *Neurology, 80*, 1778–1783.

Hill, N., Kolanowski, A. M., Milone-Nuzzo, P., & Yevchak, A. (2011). Culture change models and resident health outcomes in long-term care. *Journal of Nursing Scholarship, 43*, 30–40.

Institute of Medicine. (2012). *The mental health and substance use workforce for older adults: In whose hands.* Washington, DC: National Academy of Sciences.

Kaiser Family Foundation. (2014a). *Eligibility and cost containment policies used in Medicaid HCBS Programs.* Retrieved from http://kff.org/report-section/medicaid-home-and-community-based-services-programs-2010-data-update-eligibility-and-cost-containment-policies-used-in-medicaid-hcbs-programs/

Kaiser Family Foundation. (2014b). *Medicaid spending growth in the great recession and its aftermath, FY 2007–2012.* Retrieved from http://kff.org/report-section/medicaid-spending-growth-in-the-great-recession-issue-brief/

Kaiser Health News. (2011). *Medicare rule sparks concerns about patients' access to home health care.* Retrieved from http://www.kaiserhealthnews.org/stories/2011/march/24/face-to-face-home-health-rule.aspx

Kane, R. (2010). Reimagining nursing homes; the art of the possible. *Journal of Aging & Social Policy, 22*, 321–333.

Kane, R., Lum, T., Kane, R., Homyak, P, Parashuram, & Wysocki, A. (2013). Does home and community based care affect nursing home use. *Journal of Aging & Social Policy, 25*, 146–160.

Karel, M., Gatz, M., & Smyer, M. (2012). Aging and mental health in the decade ahead: What psychologists need to know. *American Psychologist, 67*, 184–198.

Kaskie, B., Gregory, D., & Cavanaugh, J. (2008). The use of public mental health services by older Californians and complementary service system effects. *The Journal of Behavioral Health Services & Research, 35*, 142–157.

Kaskie, B., Imhof, S., & Wyatt, M. (2008). Local Medicare policies: A pathway for providing mental health services to older adults. *Psychological Services, 5*, 60–72.

Knight, B., & Sayegh, P. (2011). Mental health and aging in the 21st century. *Journal of Aging & Social Policy, 23,* 228–243.

Lee, J., Hasnain-Wynia, R. & Lau, D. (2011). Delay in seeing a doctor due to cost: Disparity between older adults with and without disabilities in the United States. *Health Services Research, 47,* 698–720.

Medicare Board of Trustees. (2013). *Annual Report.* Retrieved from https://www.cms.gov/Research-Statistics-Data-and-Systems/Statistics-Trends-and-Reports/ReportsTrustFunds/Downloads/TR2013.pdf

Medicare.gov. (2014a). *Closing the coverage gap, Medicare prescription drugs are becoming more affordable.* Retrieved from http://www.medicare.gov/pubs/pdf/11493.pdf

Medicare.gov. (2014b). *Nursing home compare.* Retrieved from http://www.medicare.gov/nursinghomecompare/search.html

Miller, E., Allen, S., & Mor, V. (2009). Commentary: navigating the labyrinth of long-term care: shoring up informal caregiving in a home and community-based world. *Journal of Aging & Social Policy, 21,* 1–16.

National Health Council. (2014). About Chronic Diseases. Retrieved from www.nationalhealthcouncil.org/NHC_Files/Pdf_Files/AboutChronicDisease.pdf

National PACE Association. (2014). *What is PACE?* Retrieved from http://www.npaonline.org/website/article.asp?id=12

Ng, T., Harrington, C., & Kitchener, M. (2010). Medicare and Medicaid in long-term care. *Health Affairs, 29,* 22–28.

Pritchard, E. (2013). Common nursing home problems and how to resolve them. *The Elder Law Report, 10,* 1–6.

Spillman, B., & Long, S. (2007). *Does high caregiver stress lead to nursing home entry?* Washington, DC: Urban Institute.

Thomas, W. H. (1996). *Life Worth Living: How someone you love can enjoy life in a nursing home. The Eden Alternative in action.* Acton, MA: VanderWyk & Burnham.

Tilly, J. (2007). *Consumer directed, home and community services for adults with dementia.* Public Policy Brief. Chicago: Alzheimer's Association.

U.S. Department of Health and Human Services, Office of Inspector General. (2012). *Personal care services. Trends, vulnerabilities and recommendations.* Retrieved from https://oig.hhs.gov/reports-and-publications/portfolio/portfolio-12-12-01.pdf

CHAPTER 6

Employment, Retirement, and Human Rights

The right to work is a fundamental right according to the Universal Declaration of Human Rights (UNDHR) Article 23 states the following: "(1) Everyone has the right to work, to free choice of employment, to just and favorable conditions of work, and to protection against unemployment; (2) everyone, without any discrimination, has the right to equal pay for equal work; (3) everyone has the right to just and favorable remuneration ensuring for himself and his family an existence worthy of human dignity, and supplemented, if necessary by other means of protection; and (4) everyone has the right to form and to join trade unions for the protection of his interests."

As America ages, so does its workforce. The percentage of the U.S. workforce aged 55 and older has increased from 29.7% in 1992 to 40.5% in 2012 (Bureau of Labor Statistics, 2013). According to data from a Gallup Poll, the average age of retirement in 2013 was 61, in comparison to 57 in the early 1990s, with 37% of non-retirees expecting to retire after age 65 as compared to 14% in 1995 (Brown, 2013, p. 3).

Concerns about finances and depleted savings have contributed to expectations to work longer, with fewer planning to retire before 65 (Coe & Haverstick, 2010; Helman, Copeland, & VanDerhei, 2011). By 2010, workers between the ages of 55 and 64 saw the value of their 401(k)s decline by one-third, causing many to put off retirement (Grossman, 2013). The impact continues to be felt, with only 26% of Americans in 2012 thinking that they will retire before age 65 as compared to 49% thinking they would do so in 1995 (as found in the Gallup Economic and Personal Finance Survey). Economics and the toll that the recession took on their resources is the primary motivation for older people to continue working (Brown, 2012). A survey conducted by AARP in 2007 found that 70% of employed adults between the ages of 45 and 74 planned to work in retirement or never retire, primarily due to concerns over financial security (AARP, 2008).

Older workers with college and advanced degrees tend to stay in the workforce longer than those with less education and have been found to be as productive as younger workers (Burtless, 2013). Some data also suggest that work, with its mental engagement, may also be protective of cognitive abilities as those who continue through their early sixties appear to have better cognitive functioning than their retired peers (Rohwedder & Willis, 2010).

TRAINING

In order to remain productive, older workers require training to keep them at par with the skills and knowledge of their younger counterparts. Unfortunately, employers are often reluctant to provide such training, mostly based on biases and stereotypes that these workers will not be able to learn new skills or that such training is not economically viable, as the individuals will be retiring soon.

Older workers thus have less access to training. However, they are likely to have more opportunities if they are highly skilled, have good work performance, and have had low rates of absenteeism (Lazazzara, Karpinska, & Henkens, 2013). A study of older workers participating in job training and their satisfaction with their work found a positive relationship between training and job satisfaction, with the two contributing to increased productivity and reduced worker turnover (Leppel, Brucker, & Cochran, 2012). The findings underscore how older workers can benefit from such training, just as their younger cohorts do (Charness & Czaja, 2006).

Factors that may encourage older workers to participate in training programs include their confidence that they will be able to succeed, social support, recognition of the benefits of the training, interest in career advancement, and general inclination to learn (Liu, Courtenay, & Valentine, 2011). Consequently, by designing programs that incorporate these factors, employers can help to increase older workers' participation. This participation benefits both the employees and employers as it helps to maintain a motivated and skilled workforce.

RETIREMENT

Retirement calls for many changes in a person's life. The transition involves a readjustment in routine, supports, and social networks. For many, it involves a reduction in income and, consequently, concerns about financial insecurity. Most persons do not financially prepare themselves for retirement. The median retirement account balance is $3,000 for all households and $12,000 for those nearing retirement, with two-thirds of those 55 to 64 years of age having retirement savings that are less than their annual income, meaning that it is far less than what they will need for a financially secure retirement (Rhee, 2013). Overall, over 40% of Americans have no retirement savings; thus, retirement becomes a financial struggle.

Lifetimes of lower earnings, part-time work, and higher unemployment contribute to lower resources in retirement for African American and Hispanic elderly. Both groups enter retirement with lower financial assets, less home equity, and less savings than White retirees (John, 2010). Older Blacks and Hispanics are also less likely to have pensions and thus tend to remain working due to economic necessity (Flippen & Tienda, 2000).

Average workers have approximately 15 years of retirement and many may spend almost a quarter of their lives retired (Adams & Rau, 2011). Research on factors associated with well-being in retirement indicates that physical health, having goals, and being flexible are critical to enjoyment (Kubicek, Korunka, Raymo, & Hoonakker, 2011). At the same time, having sufficient financial assets and feeling satisfied with one's previous work appear to be more important to men's adjustment, whereas being involved in social networks and having support may be more important to women (Kubicek, Korunka, Raymo, & Hoonakker, 2011). Overall, those with better physical health and more financial resources are likely to have better psychological well-being in retirement.

Retirement planning can be an important factor for future adjustment to the postretirement period as it assists with the transition. Persons are better prepared for the transition by anticipating what to expect and by learning about options. The importance of retirement planning is underscored by findings from the Health and Retirement Study (National Institute on Aging, 2014), which shows that even thinking about retirement and discussing it can significantly ease the transition. In addition to helping with financial planning, programs should also help individuals develop goals and ideas for activities in retirement. People should also consider what they are looking forward to and what makes them anxious about retirement. Information on leisure and volunteer activities, as well as housing options, should also be covered since they are subjects that can be important to postretirement adjustment.

The New York State Program begins with self-assessment and continues to goal setting, information gathering, actions, then terminates with reviewing and updating. Planning is seen as a constant process in which people are continually involved as there is a definite relationship between planning and a satisfying retirement (New York State Office on Aging, 2014).

Since retirement planning can be a factor in adjustment, it is troubling that few people actually prepare for the transition. In fact, a study of over 12,000 people in 12 countries, including the United States, found that only 20% of employees had any real understanding of financial issues related to retirement (Transamerica Center for Retirement Studies, 2014). Specific to the United States, research on more than 200 companies regarding the use of their retirement plans indicates that employees do not fully understand existing retirement plans and are generally unengaged and unprepared for retirement (Gillespie, 2012). At the same time, although most employees reported that they were interested in more information and even financial counseling, only one in ten accepted the advice that was offered. Most disturbing is the finding that persons with higher income are the most likely to partake in retirement planning and in anticipating retirement (Curl & Ingram, 2013). Consequently, those with fewer resources and who may be in great need of such programs are least likely to access them. In addition, even when employers offer plans, ethnic and minority employees have very low participation rates in comparison to their White peers (Kujawa, 2010).

Mandatory Retirement

Mandatory retirement requires an employee to retire at a specific age, irrespective of whether he or she wishes to continue working. With amendments to the Age Discrimination Employment Act (ADEA), such forced retirement was made illegal. Thus, in 1986, it became illegal in almost all areas of employment to force people to retire at a certain age. The groups excepted from the Law are public safety-related jobs that have physical and cognitive fitness requirements such as air traffic controllers, who must retire at age 56, and airline pilots, who must retire at age 61. For federal law enforcement personnel, the mandatory retirement age is 57. In addition, companies such as law firms and accounting firms can set retirement ages that cause highly paid employees with major responsibilities to retire at 60 or 65.

The underlying belief is that skills and abilities decline after the age of 65 with persons unable to adequately perform their jobs. However, without actually evaluating each individual employee, mandatory retirement is in fact age discrimination as age alone is used as an indicator of competency. Not surprisingly, being forced to retire has been related to lower psychological well-being in retirement (van Solinge & Henkens, 2008).

AGE DISCRIMINATION

The ADEA of 1967 is a federal law that protects workers age 40 and over from age-based discrimination in hiring and in employment. Employees are protected with regard to hiring, firing, layoffs, pay, benefits, promotions, demotions, performance reviews, and other conditions of employment. Age cannot be stated as a criterion for recruitment, age limits cannot be set on training programs, employers cannot retaliate against those charging age discrimination, and mandated retirement is narrowly restricted to a few occupations. Since 2009, workers have also had to prove that age was the decisive reason for their discrimination. In contrast, those charging discrimination due to reasons such as race, gender, or disability have to only prove the one factor as a cause. The Act applies to employers with at least 20 employees, while most state laws apply to employers with fewer than 20 employees.

Sixty-four percent of workers between the ages of 45 and 74 claim that they have experienced age discrimination at work, and 93% of those say that it is common (AARP, 2014). Between 2006 and 2013, age discrimination claims rose to 38% (Mukherji, 2013), but proving discrimination is difficult. The plaintiff must show that age is the main or motivating factor in not being hired or in being dismissed.

The Equal Employment Opportunity Commission (EEOC) is responsible for investigating all claims of age discrimination and resolving them. Cases are then closed either due to administrative reasons or because there was insufficient evidence of discrimination. Data from the EEOC for 2013 show that of 21,396 cases that they received, 16.3% were closed due to administrative reasons and 69% were found to have no reasonable cause. Only 2.8% were found to have "reasonable cause" of discrimination (EEOC, 2014). Consequently, it remains difficult for an employee to prove age discrimination, and older workers and job seekers remain vulnerable to dismissal.

OLDER WORKERS AND UNEMPLOYMENT

Older workers were particularly affected by the recession of 2008. In 2007, less than one in four unemployed older workers was out of work for more than 6 months; in 2011, more than half faced long-term unemployment (U.S. Government Accounting Office [GAO], 2012b). Moreover, when rehired, their median earnings were only 85% of their previous earnings as compared to 95% for younger workers. At the same time, the recession made it more difficult to prove age discrimination due to disruptions in the marketplace and uncertain demands about future employment needs (Newmark & Button, 2013). It was all the more difficult to prove that age was a decisive factor, with fewer available jobs and more people competing for the same. In addition, as most job applications are submitted online with no personal contact, it is difficult to prove that age is a segregating factor in hiring. Some employers even require that applicants enter their birthdate on their online application, not permitting them to continue to the next page without it.

Reasons for not being able to find employment include out-of-date skills, discouragement, and depression that can impact interviews, as well as inexperience with online applications (GAO, 2012b). Other barriers include employers' reluctance to hire those who had earned higher salaries previously, managers who believe the person would be unhappy working for a younger manager, fears of expensive health benefits, and beliefs that the person will be retiring soon so it is not worth providing expensive training. However, it is also important to note that workers 65 and older have the lowest incidence of any age group of occupational injuries (Bureau of Labor Statistics, 2013).

Once out of employment, older adults, those over 55, have a much more difficult time finding reemployment than those who are younger. Data from the U.S. Department of Labor (2013) show those over the age of 55 have an average duration of unemployment of 54 weeks as compared to 36 weeks for those under the age of 55. Although most older people out of the labor force say that they do not want a job, approximately 1.6 million said they did want a job but could not find one (Rix, 2013).

EMPLOYERS' ATTITUDES TOWARD OLDER WORKERS

Many employers maintain negative stereotypes of older employees, which act as barriers to their being hired. Compared with younger workers, older workers are perceived as less motivated, less willing to engage in training and career development programs, more resistant to change, not as trusting, more likely to experience health problems that impact their work, and more vulnerable to work–family conflicts. A meta-analysis of 380 published empirical studies from the early 1970s through 2011 found support for only one of the stereotypes: Older workers were less likely to partake in development programs, which could be partially explained by the programs being skewed toward younger employees (Ng & Feldman, 2012).

Employers are also concerned that older workers may be less creative, less willing to take initiative, less willing to learn, and less able to perform physically demanding jobs (Munnell, Sass, & Soto, 2006). In addition, they are concerned that they are more expensive, as they are paid more and health insurance costs increase with age. On the positive side, older workers are described as valued due to their experience, knowledge, work habits, attitudes, commitment, loyalty, punctuality, and respect (Dennis & Thomas, 2007). The loss of their expertise, skills, and knowledge can seriously impact many companies. Moreover, for some, age is actually perceived as an advantage, with older employees being more productive, although more expensive, than those who are younger (Munnell, Sass, & Soto, 2006).

Of particular concern to many employers is the issue of Alzheimer's disease and related disorders (ADRD) in older employees and the question of how to respond to it (Babcock, 2009). With people continuing to delay retirement and the aging of the workforce, the risk of cognitive impairment among employees increases. According to the Alzheimer's Association, the number of people affected by ADRD will increase 350% by the middle of the century (Alzheimer's Association, 2011). Many of those affected will still be employed and often it is at work that symptoms such as memory loss, forgetfulness, and disorientation are first noticed. One employment assistance professional (EAP) reported that since 2009, calls related to Alzheimer's in the workplace had increased 100%, which he attributed to the recession and the need for people to continue to work (Kaylin, 2011).

A study of human resource professionals in 103 companies found that they were unsure how to recognize symptoms of impairment and how to respond to them. They also felt that further training with regard to dementia was important, with more education on how to provide assistance to those with symptoms (Cox & Pardasani, 2013). Providing such training is critical to assuring that the rights of those who are impaired are supported. Many can continue to work and be productive even with some impairment. Dismissing employees on the basis of their impairment can be a violation of the Americans with Disabilities Act (ADA) and of their human rights.

The legal profession has also shown concern about the aging of its profession and the increasing risk of more lawyers with age-related impairments and insufficient preparation for transitioning away from practice (www.nobc.org). Aging lawyers present challenges to the profession, as any impairment in cognitive functioning can seriously impact the lawyers' ability to fully perform their roles. In dealing with this concern, jurisdictions are encouraged to develop programs for early detection of lessening skills, provide assistance to those who are impaired, and assure that senior lawyers are treated with respect and share their wisdom with new lawyers. The profession is designing guidelines that protect the rights of the attorneys and the profession itself.

PENDING LEGISLATION

Fair Employment Opportunity Act of 2011

The Fair Employment Opportunity Act of 2011 is intended to assist older workers seeking employment. Employers often discriminate against those who have been unemployed for long periods of time. This can be a major barrier to the employment of older adults as they are likely to spend longer periods unemployed; consequently, this bill would indirectly benefit them. Under the Act, employers would not be able to refuse or not consider hiring qualified people simply because they are unemployed or to favor those who are currently working. The Act was referred to the Committee in January 2013 and is yet to be acted upon.

Protecting Older Americans Against Discrimination Act

The Protecting Older Americans Against Discrimination Act was introduced into Congress in March 2012 but still remains in committee. The Act would strengthen protections for older workers by ending the requirement for burdens of proof in employment discrimination cases, as well as the need to show that age was one discriminating factor along with other factors in employment decisions. The present law allows employers the freedom to discriminate against older workers by enabling them to confound motives and other reasons with age. The Act would strengthen the claims of employees in that they would only have to show that age was a factor in any decision made by the employer, making it easier to prove discrimination.

Older Women, Employment, and Retirement

Women's participation in the labor force continues to grow and this expansion continues through later adulthood. Between 1975 and 2010, the rate of women, age 55 and older, in the labor force increased from 23% to 35%, while that of men decreased from 49% to 46% during the same period (Copeland, 2011). At the same time, women were more likely than men to be working part-time.

The 2008 recession had considerable effects on women's employment. Between 2007 and 2011, unemployment for women 55–64 rose from 3% to 6.1%, and rose from 2.1% to 6.5% for those 65 and over. In comparison to men, who regained 34% of the jobs that they lost during this period, women regained only 23%. Of the vast majority of jobs created during the period, 90% went to men (Johnson, 2012).

When employed, women still struggle with a gender gap with regard to wages; this gap increases with age. Between the ages of 35 and 44, women who work full time receive approximately 80% of men's earnings, decreasing to approximately 76% for those aged 65 and over (U.S. Department of Labor, 2010). With lifetimes of lower earnings that are also reflected in lower Social Security benefits, it is not surprising that older women face retirement with less financial security than older men (Hayes & Hartman, 2011) and greater financial worries (Rix, 2012; U.S. Department of Labor, 2010). This insecurity is compounded by the fact that when faced with unemployment, older women are likely to take early Social Security benefits, which means that their continued benefits will be lower than if they had delayed taking them until full retirement age.

The financial well-being of older women is also impacted by their caregiving responsibilities, which significantly impact their retirement income. Nearly two-thirds of the 54 million caregivers in the United States are women and most are actively in it while they are still employed (MetLife, 2011). However, only a minority have flexible work hours that can compensate for their caregiving activities, and many are unable to take advantage of flexible schedules out of fear that it would hinder their promotions. According to MetLife, nearly 80% of those eligible for the Family Medical Leave Act (FMLA) did not take it, as they could not afford unpaid leave (MetLife, 2011). The result is that the average woman over 50 who reduces employment due to caregiving loses more than $185,000 in salary and Social Security benefits, whereas those who leave employment lose over $324,044 in wages, Social Security, and pensions (MetLife, 2011).

The outcome of reduced income, less access to pensions, and interrupted work histories results in lower retirement savings and income for women. Women remain at greater financial risk with more women (69%) compared to men (57%) dependent on Social Security benefits for the majority of their income (Transamerica, 2013). It is thus not surprising that in retirement, older men report annual incomes that are nearly 75% higher than an older woman's (Wider Opportunities for Women [WOW], 2012). Thus, in 2012, the median income of older women was $15,323 while that of older men was $27,656 (Women's Institute for a Secure Retirement [WISER], 2014). Moreover, with longer life spans, women are at greater risk of outliving their savings and income.

In 1988, in recognition of the issues that women often face at retirement, the Administration on Aging established the National Resource Center on Women and Retirement Planning. The Center develops financial and retirement materials specifically for women, and particularly targets average- and low-income minority or "underserved" women who are most likely to be vulnerable economically in retirement with less access to any retirement program. The Women's Institute for a Secure Retirement (WISER), founded in 1996 by the Heinz Family Philanthropies, works with the Center in conducting research on the economic situation of older women and provides them with basic financial information for retirement planning.

SUMMARY

The right to work without discrimination and the right to security with adequate resources and financial protection are fundamental human rights. Although policies to protect these rights exist, they remain hampered in their effectiveness. Age remains a factor in mandatory retirement, layoffs, length of unemployment, and hiring. Age discrimination also occurs when older employees are not offered the same training opportunities available to those who are younger. Until age is no longer a factor in employment practices, the rights of older adults are at risk. Concerns about these rights are underscored in pending legislation such as the *Fair Employment Opportunity Act* and *Protecting Older Americans Against Discrimination Act,* both of which would promote and sustain older employees in the workplace.

Making the workplace more amenable to older workers through more flextime, part-time, and even telecommuting could enable many to continue working for longer periods. Such adjustments may be particularly critical for women who are often juggling employment with caregiving roles. Ensuring that older people participate in training programs and that their skills are congruent with those of younger persons is important both for employees and employers. At the same time, their continued participation means continued federal tax contributions and fewer persons depending on Social Security and private pension plans.

Dealing with the negative biases and stereotypes that many employers hold about older workers is essential for helping to overcome discrimination. As long as employers believe that older workers cost more than they can produce, that their skills are not updated, and that they cannot benefit from training, ageism will continue. Programs that assist employers in recognizing the importance of experience and commitment may help to change perceptions and practices. In the same way, programs that educate employers about ADRD and how to deal with it in the workplace can help to assure that the rights and dignity of impaired employees are upheld.

Special attention must also be given to employees who may be showing symptoms of cognitive impairment. Without an understanding of the symptoms and how they may impact work, the rights of impaired employees are vulnerable. It is imperative that with the aging of the workforce, employers receive education and training on cognitive impairment and ADRD, and on how to counsel and support these employees to assure that their rights are not violated.

Retirement planning can be an important component of a successful retirement. Planning needs to encompass both financial and psychological preparation for the transition. Policies should assure the availability and accessibility of these programs to all employees so that they can be informed and take appropriate measures before retirement actually occurs. Assuring that employees are informed and have taken the appropriate planning steps can help assure their adjustment and security in retirement. Such planning should also go beyond financial issues and encompass lifestyle concerns and changes that commonly occur with retirement. By anticipating what to expect and preparing for it, people may be better able to deal with changes that retirement commonly brings.

The critical need for retirement savings, particularly among low- and middle-income workers, was addressed in a proposal (MyRa) put forth by President Obama in 2014. Under this proposal, workers could have part of their pay deducted for deposit in a retirement account invested in U.S. government bonds, which would be treated like an individual retirement account. Initial investments would be low and the plans would be open to those with incomes up to $191,000. The plan gives important recognition to the plight faced by many older Americans as they wrestle with financial solvency in retirement. It also underscores the need to improve access to retirement plans that can help to assure their savings and income for future security.

As discussed, retirement can be particularly challenging for women, who continue to struggle with insufficient income and assets. The inequality that they experience throughout their working life takes its toll on their retirement. Among the suggestions for improving women's financial well-being in retirement are requiring employers to enroll employees in an Individual Retirement Plan (IRA); offering a tax credit for retirement savings; allowing caregivers to contribute to IRAs; strengthening spousal protections in IRA accounts; increasing the duration of unemployment benefits, which could prevent workers from applying for early Social Security benefits; and proposals that would help to ensure that women have an adequate income in retirement, such as updating the Social Security Survivor's benefit (GAO, 2012a). Such adjustments could improve the financial status and security of women in retirement and further support their human rights.

Finally, from a human rights perspective, it is imperative to offer older adults options regarding employment and retirement. Not everyone will want to continue working or may be able to; however, for those who do want to continue, age must not be a deciding factor. Concomitantly, retirement should be a personal choice and entered into with an understanding of what it entails, including its opportunities and challenges. Widening opportunities for both employment and retirement is fundamental to assuring the dignity and development of older adults.

QUESTIONS FOR DISCUSSION

1. Discuss some of the main reasons impacting the right to work for older adults.

2. How does mandatory retirement relate to human rights? What are your own beliefs about it?

3. Discuss some of the reasons why older adults may face longer periods of unemployment than younger workers. How does this impact them?

4. What factors impact women's retirement? What measures could be done to ease their retirement?

REFERENCES

AARP. (2008). *Staying ahead of the curve 2007: The AARP work and career study.* Washington, DC: Author.

Adams, G., & Rau, B. (2011). Putting off tomorrow to do what you want today: Planning for retirement. *American Psychologist, 66,* 180–192.

Alzheimer's Association. (2011). *Facts about Alzheimer's disease, elder care and the workplace.* Fact Sheet. Chicago: Alzheimer's Association.

American Association of Retired Persons. (2014). *Staying ahead of the curve 2013: The AARP work and career study.* Washington, DC: AARP.

Babcock, P. (2009). *Avoid assumptions about Alzheimer's.* Society for Human Resource Management, Discipline articles.

Brown, S. (2012). *What are older workers seeking: An AARP/SHRM survey of 50+ workers.* Washington, DC: AARP Research.

Brown, A. (2013). In U.S. average retirement age up to 61. Gallup poll briefing, 5/13/2013.

Bureau of Labor Statistics. (2013). *Labor force projections to 2022: The labor force participation rate continues to fall.* Monthly Labor Review. Washington, DC: Department of Labor.

Bureau of Labor Statistics. (2013). U.S. Department of Labor. *The Editor's Desk. Older workers less likely to have severe work injuries, but they miss more work days to recover.* Retrieved from http://www.bls.gov/opub/ted/2013/ted_20131230.htm

Burtless, G. (2013). *The impact of population aging and delayed retirement on work-force productivity.* Chestnut Hill, MA: Center for Retirement Research at Boston College.

Charness, N., & Czaja, S. J. (2006). *Older worker training: What we know and don't know.* AARP Public Policy Institute, No. 22. Washington, DC: AARP. Retrieved from http://assets.aarp.org/rgcenter/econ/2006_22_worker.pdf

Coe, N. B., & Haverstick, K. (2010). *How do responses to the downturn vary by household characteristics?* Issue Brief No. 10–17. Chestnut Hill, MA: Center for Retirement Research at Boston College.

Copeland, C. (2011). Labor force participation rates of the population age 55 and older: What did the recession do to the trends? *EBRI Notes, 32,* 82–86.

Cox, C., & Pardasani, M. (2013). Alzheimer's in the workplace: A challenge for social work. *Journal of Gerontological Social Work, 56,* 643–656.

Curl, A., & Ingram, J. (2013). Anticipatory socialization for retirement: A multilevel dyadic model. *Clinical Gerontologist, 36,* 375–393.

Dennis, H., & Thomas, K. (2007). Ageism in the workplace. *Generations, 31,* 84.

Flippen, C., & Tienda, M. (2000). Pathways to retirement: Patterns of labor force participation and labor market exit among the pre-retirement population by race, Hispanic origin, and sex. *Journal of Gerontology, B-Psychology, 55B,* S14–S27.

Gillespie, L. (2012). Gap between employer, employee views on retirement. *Employee Benefit News, 26,* 21–22.

Government Accounting Office (GAO). (2012a). *Retirement security—Women still face challenges.* GAO-12-699.

Government Accounting Office (GAO). (2012b). *Unemployed older workers; many experience challenges regaining employment and face reduced retirement security.* GAO-12-4445.

Grossman, R. (2013). Invest in older workers. *Human Resource Magazine, 58.* Society for Human Resource Managers (SHRM), Alexandria.

Hayes, J., & Hartman, H. (2011). *Living on the edge: Economic insecurity after the Great Recession, September 2011.* New York: Institute for Women's Policy Research & Rockefeller Survey of Economic Security.

Helman, R., Copeland, C., & VanDerhei, J. (2011). *The 2011 Retirement Confidence Survey: Confidence drops to record lows, reflecting "the new normal."* Issue Brief No. 355. Washington, DC: Employee Benefit Research Institute.

John, D. (2010). *Disparities for women and minorities in retirement saving.* Washington, DC: Brookings.

Johnson, R. (2012). *Older workers, retirement and the Great Recession.* Stanford, CA: Stanford Center on Poverty and Inequality.

Kaylin, A. (2011). *Older workforce, new problems: Alzheimer's in the workplace.* Livonia, MI: American Society of Employers.

Kubicek, B., Korunka, C., Raymo, J., & Hoonakker, P. (2011). Psychological well-being in retirement: The effects of personal and gendered contextual resources. *Journal of Occupational Health Psychology, 16,* 230–246.

Kujawa, P. (2010). Minorities still lagging retirement participation. *Workforce Management, 89*(2), 10–11.

Lazazzara, A., Karpinska, K., & Henkens, K. (2013). What factors influence training opportunities for older workers? Three factorial surveys exploring the attitudes of HR professionals. *International Journal of Human Resource Management, 24,* 2154–2172.

Leppel, K., Brucker, E., & Cochran, J. (2012). The importance of job training to job satisfaction of older workers. *Journal of Aging & Social Policy, 24,* 62–76.

Liu, S., Courtenay, G., & Valentine, T. (2011). Managing older worker training: A literature review and conceptual framework. *Educational Gerontology, 37,* 1040–1062.

MetLife Mature Market Institute. (2011). *The MetLife study of caregiving costs to working caregivers: Double jeopardy for baby boomers caring for their parents.* Retrieved from http://www.metlife.com/assets/cao/mmi/publications/ studies/2011/mmi-caregiving-costs-working-caregivers.pdf

Mukherji, A. (2013). *EEOC Age-discrimination claims up 38% in 6 years.* Retrieved from http://blogs.findlaw.com/law_and_life/2013/12/eeoc-age-discrimination-claims-up-38-in-6-years.html

Munnell, A., Sass, S., & Soto, M. (2006). *Employer attitudes towards older workers: Survey results.* Work opportunities for older Americans Series 3. Chestnut Hill, MA: Center for Retirement Research at Boston College.

National Institute on Aging (2014) *Growing older in America: The health and retirement study.* Retrieved from http://www.nia.nih.gov/health/publication/growing-older-america-health-and-retirement-study/chapter-2-work-and-retirement

Newmark, D., & Button, P. (2013). *Did age discrimination protections help older workers weather the great recession?* National Bureau of Economic Research, Working Paper 19216. Washington, DC: NBER.

New York State Office on Aging. (2014). *Pre-retirement planning self-help guide for New York State employees.* Retrieved from http://www.worklife.ny.gov/preretirement/selfhelpguide/index.html

Ng, T., & Feldman, D. (2012). Evaluating six common stereotypes about older workers with meta-analytical data. *Personnel Psychology, 65.* Retrieved from http://www.strategy-business.com/emailarticle?url=www.strategy-business.com/article/re00225&ids=27802017-31283745

NOBC-APRL-CoLAP. (2014). Second Joint Committee on Aging Lawyers. Retrieved from http://www.nobc.org/docs/news/NOBC-APRL-CoLAP-final-report.pdf

Rhee, N. (2013). *The retirement savings crisis: Is it worse than we think?* Washington, DC: National Institute on Retirement Security.

Rix, S. (2012). *Boomer women feeling more financially insecure than men.* Fact Sheet No. 269. Washington, DC: AARP. Retrieved from http://www.aarp.org/content/dam/aarp/research/public_policy_institute/econ_sec/2012/boomer-women-feeling-financially-insecure-AARP-ppi-econ-sec.pd

Rix, S. (2013). *The employment situation, May 2013: Some good news for older workers tempered by continuing problems.* Fact Sheet No. 284. AARP Public Policy Institute. Washington, DC: Author.

Rohwedder, S. & Willis, R. (2010). Mental Retirement. *Journal Ecoomic Perspectives, 24,* 119–138.

Transamerica Center for Retirement Studies. (2013). *Juggling current needs and long-term security: Every women needs her own retirement.* Retrieved from http://www.transamericacenter.org/docs/default-source/resources/center research/TCRS2013_SR_women.pdf

Transamerica Center for Retirement Studies. (2014). *New study finds workers around the world are unprepared for retirement.* Transamerica Center for Retirement Studies: Author.

U.S. Department of Labor. (2010). *Highlights of women's earnings in 2009*. Report No. 1025. Washington, DC: Author.

U.S. Department of Labor. (2013). *Labor for statistics*. Retrieved from http://www.bls.gov/opub/ee/archive.htm

U.S. Equal Employment Opportunity Commission (EEOC). (2014). Age Discrimination in Employment Act, FY 1997-FY 2013. Retrieved from http://www.eeoc.gov/eeoc/statistics/enforcement/adea.cfm

van Solinge, H., & Henkens, K. (2008). Adjustment to and satisfaction with retirement: Two of a kind? *Psychology and Aging, 23,* 422–434.

Wider Opportunities for Women (WOW). (2012). *Doing without: Economic insecurity and older Americans*. No. 2. Author. Retrieved from http://www.wowonline.org/documents/OlderAmericansGenderbriefFINAL.pdf

Women's Institute for a Secure Retirement (WISER). (2014). *The pay gap's connected to the retirement gap*. Retrieved from http://www.wiserwomen.org/index.php?id=266&page=pay-gap-retirement-gap

CHAPTER 7

Policy, Family, and Human Rights

The Universal Declaration of Human Rights attests to the rights of the family (Article 16) as the natural and fundamental group in society entitled to protection by the society and the State. The role of the family does not decline as people age; rather, it may increase in importance. Four in ten adults in the United States are caring for family members who need assistance with functioning (National Alliance for Caregiving [NAC] & AARP, 2009). Thus, contrary to the myth that older people become isolated, most age within family networks with spouse, family, or friends, who are significant factors in their well-being (Antonucci, Birditt, & Webster, 2010). Moreover, family support is the critical factor in enabling many older persons to remain in their own homes and within the community.

In 2009, about 42.1 million family caregivers assisted an adult each day with limitations in physical activities and 61.6 million provide some care during the year (NAC & AARP, 2009). The importance of this care is highlighted by findings that show having a spouse, daughter, or sibling significantly reduced the risk of nursing home entry. Being married reduces the risk of entering a nursing home by 41%, having at least one daughter reduces the risk by 27%, and having at least one living sibling reduces the risk by 21% (Freedman, 1996).

Data from the National Long-Term Care Survey show that 85% of these older care recipients received care from their spouse or children (Houser, Gibson, & Redfoot, 2010). Most significant with regard to the care these persons provide is that only 1% of persons with these relationships and care needs received assistance from a formal agency. A troubling finding with regard to the receipt of formal care assistance provided by an agency is that there was an actual decline in its use between 1994 and 2004 while needs for care did not change. Consequently, family caregivers assumed many of the care tasks that had been provided by formal agencies. The decline in the receipt of formal care was highest among spouses with no children and those with limitations in five or six activities of daily living (ADLs).

Among the tasks performed by family caregivers are those associated with ADLs, such as eating, bathing, dressing, toileting, and transferring from bed to chair, as well as the instrumental activities of daily living (IADLs), such as transportation, shopping, housework, managing medications, and meal preparation. Data on caregivers for older adults show that they spend an average of 19 hours per week providing assistance, with one in five providing more than 40 hours per week (NAC & AARP, 2009). The average length of time for providing this care is almost four and a half years, although caregiving for dementia can range from 4 to 20 years (NAC & AARP, 2009).

Families are increasingly caring for those with more disabilities and those who are older, factors that can add to caregiving demands and stress. As the functional status of the relative declines, the tasks and roles that caregivers assume expand. Moreover, many of these caregivers are themselves vulnerable. The NAC and AARP survey found 63% of caregivers were 75 or older, with the majority being women and the majority of the care being provided to older women. Supporting these family caregivers is critical for their own well-being and that of their older relative.

WHY DO PEOPLE CARE?

Reciprocity is often given as a motive for helping and providing care to an older adult. According to the norm of reciprocity, people feel obligated to assist those who have cared for them at various points in their lives. To not reciprocate such care is to recant on a normative responsibility. An estimated 83% of Americans say they would feel very obligated to provide assistance to their parents in a time of need (Pew Research Center, 2010). As such, reciprocity provides a basis for social relationships, in that each person in the dyad is expected to both give and receive assistance. In caring for an older relative, the spouse and children are the ones most likely to be bound by this norm. However, even distant relatives may perceive their caregiving activities as a means of repaying a long-standing debt to their older relative.

Persons also become caregivers out of default—no one else is available to assume the role (Radina, 2007). Others assume the role because of loss of social networks and ties by the parents (Pope, Kolomer, & Glass, 2012). Sharing gender and similar values with the patient, emotional closeness, history of exchange, and availability also affect the decision to become a caregiver (Pillemer & Suitor, 2006). At the same time, caregivers who feel they have no choice in the decision are more likely to experience stress and strain.

Feelings of commitment and affection also motivate caregivers. These sentiments underlie many helping relationships and remain strong regardless of the distance between people or social class (Litwak, 1985). The affection transmitted through the relationship is also important for the well-being of the older person, as it reinforces their social involvement and esteem (Antonnucci & Depner, 1982).

However, the demands engendered in the caregiving relationship can also have negative effects on both the caregiver and the receiver. A failure to respond to the needs of the impaired individual can result in feelings of guilt in many family members. These feelings, and the need to compensate for them, may influence the caregivers' involvement. In those instances where there is no improvement in the condition of the dependent relative, regardless of the amount of assistance, the guilt can be hard to overcome, particularly among those whose traditional values strongly influence family care (Lim, Cheah, Noorhazlina, & Han, 2014).

Caregiving impacts the care receiver as it does the caregiver. Thus, the level of stress experienced by the caregiver is influenced by his or her assessment of the situation. At the same time, as the care receiver assesses the situation and feels able to contribute to the family, his or her sense of control increases along with psychological well-being. Being able to give as well as receive can empower the care receiver as well as the caregiver and strengthen the relationship. This empowerment is also instrumental in contributing to the rights of the receiver as it underscores his or her own personhood and social capital.

Further research on the didactic relationship between caregivers and care receivers indicates that caregivers are likely to perceive the care recipient as more dependent than persons perceive themselves (Lyons, Zarit, Sayer, & Whitlatch, 2002). In addition, as caregivers experience more strain in the caregiving relationship, they experience greater caregiver difficulties. Disagreements between the caregiver and the receiver regarding the situation and its demands can be a source of stress to both.

Traditional cultural norms can greatly influence the caring relationship. Values associated with filial piety that demand respect for the elders and the responsibility of the family in providing care to dependent relatives remain strong among many ethnic groups. Relatives who do not adhere to such behaviors are in danger of being treated as deviants from their immediate cultural groups. Moreover, to the extent that they themselves maintain these traditional values, they are susceptible to increased stress and even increased risks to their own health if they feel they are not completely fulfilling their expected caregiving roles (Giselle & Cruess, 2011).

These normative behaviors are frequently reinforced by older persons who continue to both expect and demand assistance from their children and other relatives. For these families, using any type of formal service may be interpreted as failing to fulfill one's responsibility. Consequently, in attempting to understand caregiving activities, it is essential to examine the traditional values and expectations of both the caregiver and receiver.

IMPACT ON CAREGIVERS

In comparison to non-caregivers, caregivers report more physical and mental health problems than non-caregivers, including more doctor visits, anxiety and depression, and weight loss (Ho, Chan, Woo, Chong, &

Sham, 2009). Specific groups appear to be most susceptible to negative outcomes and emotional stress (NAC & AARP, 2009). These include females, those with poor health or a high level of burden, those living with the care recipient, and those caring for someone with Alzheimer's disease and related disorders (ADRD). Caregivers with less than a college degree, an unsupportive work culture, and first-generation immigrants also express the burden associated with caregiving (Lahale, Earle, & Heymann, 2013). High levels of strain among caregivers has been found to be the factor most likely to impact their psychological well-being (Roth, Perkins, Wadlety, Temple, & Haley, 2009), with stress among caregivers being a major predictor of nursing home placement (Spillman & Long, 2009). Overall, women report more negative effects from caregiving than men (Pinquart & Sörensen, 2006).

Since Alzheimer's disease has a formidable impact on caregivers, much of the research on caregivers has focused on those caring for relatives with ADRD. Studies comparing caregiving spouses and adult children find that the illness can have particularly deleterious effects on the health and mental well-being of spouses who must deal with the daily stress associated with caregiving. This stress is exacerbated by the fact that they frequently have little respite from caregiving and must deal with the realization that they are losing a key intimate relationship in their lives (Savundranqyagam, Hummert, Montgomery, Braun, 2009).

The decision to institutionalize a relative is generally a very difficult one for caregivers. Most older persons express a profound desire to remain at home and caregivers try to adhere to these wishes as long as possible. A meta-review of 782 studies, which examined factors predicting nursing home placement for persons with dementia, found that the greater emotional stress of the caregivers, a desire to institutionalize, and feelings of being "trapped" in care responsibilities increased the likelihood of placement (Gaugler, Duval, Anderson, & Kane, 2007).

These findings are substantiated by findings from a longitudinal study of over 5,000 caregivers that found more than 40% of the persons with dementia who, at baseline, were being cared for at home and entered a nursing home during the 3-year study period . Both the burden experienced by the caregiver and the behavioral/psychiatric symptoms of the parent or spouse receiving care contributed to the institutionalization.

The findings also indicated that interventions for these families had to treat both the burden experienced by the caregiver and the symptoms of the care receiver (Gaugler, Wall, Kane, & Menk, 2011).

POLICIES THAT SUPPORT FAMILY CAREGIVERS

Given the major roles that families play in supporting older persons and helping them to remain in the community, they have a paucity of support. The major federal policies that provide assistance for caregivers are the National Family Caregiver Support Program (NFCSP) under Title III-E of the Older Americans Act, the Family and Medical Leave Act (FMLA), and The Lifespan Respite Care Act enacted by Congress in 2006 to develop a network of respite programs at state and local levels for planned or emergency respite care.

The National Family Caregiver Support Program

The NFCSP was enacted in 2000 to provide grants to states to help them support family caregivers. The program recognizes the major role that families play in providing care, as well as the stress they commonly encounter. The range of services provided include information about services; assistance to caregivers in gaining access to services; individual counseling; organization of support groups and caregiver training; respite care; and limited supplemental services. The goal of the program is to reduce caregiver depression, anxiety, and stress so that caregivers can continue to provide care and thus delay the need for institutionalization. Those eligible for the program are informal caregivers providing care to persons over the age of 60, those providing care to persons with Alzheimer's disease or another form of dementia, and grandparents caring for children under 18 years or caring for adults with disabilities.

Data on the program from 2010 show that the primary service provided was access assistance, with over 1 million contacts; counseling and training was provided to 125,000 caregivers; and respite was offered to 64,000 caregivers (Administration on Aging [AOA], 2012). Those receiving the services reported that they were very satisfied and that the assistance enabled them to provide care for a longer period of time. Approximately 12% of the family caregivers receiving some type of support were grandparents caring for a grandchild.

The NFCSP is being evaluated to determine its effectiveness in achieving client outcomes. The impact of the program on the family and the persons for whom they provide care is being assessed. Three specific areas are being studied: the access that it provides to caregivers and the systems that are needed for such access; the outcomes on caregivers and care receivers; and the program's contribution to the efficiency of the long-term care system, including cost savings by helping families to delay institutionalization (AOA, 2013).

The latest estimate of the value of the care and services that family caregivers provide is $450 billion annually (Feinberg, Reinhard, Houser, & Choula, 2011), while the latest appropriations for the Act (FY 2013) were $143.6 million, an amount that has changed very little since 2001 (Napili & Colello, 2013). With approximately 65.7 million caregivers in the United States each caregiver is entitled to approximately $233 per year through the program. Given the nature, length of time, and extent of the tasks associated with caregiving, the ability of the program to really impact the lives of these caregivers is questionable.

A further barrier impacting the overall effectiveness of the program is its variations among states. States with a history of providing caregiver support services are more likely to provide services under the NFCSP, which may be due to their ability to identify and serve the caregiver's needs (Giunta, 2010). The program also suffers from the fact that many are not aware of it, cultural or linguistic barriers, and a lack of uniform assessment tools (Buhler-Wilkerson, 2007; Koerin, Harrigan, & Secret, 2008; Scharlach, Dal Santo, Lehning, et al., 2006). Consequently, many who could benefit remain excluded.

Lifespan Respite Care Act

One of the most pressing needs for caregivers is respite, that is, temporary relief from caregiving. It is usually provided at home but is also provided in a nursing home where persons leave their relative for a short time. As part of a long-term care system, it can provide support to family caregivers, which can potentially enable them to continue caregiving for longer periods of time.

The Lifespan Respite Care Act was passed in 2006 as part of the Public Health Service Act. With its "lifes pan" approach, it is not limited to one age group but serves caregivers of both children and adults with disabilities. The Act provides funds to state agencies to develop or improve respite activities; improve the dissemination of information about respite or improve coordination; and provide, supplement, or improve access and quality of services. Between 2007 and 2011, grants were awarded to 30 states with a total appropriation of $289 million. In FY 2011, the Lifespan Respite Care Program was funded at just under $2.5 million and funding has not changed since then (Napili & Colello, 2013). Consequently, its ability to support families remains very limited.

The Family and Medical Leave Act

The FMLA of 1993 is the only federal law that deals specifically with employed caregivers and thus reflects Article 23 of the Universal Declaration of Human Rights (UNDHR), the right to work and to do so without discrimination. It enables family caregivers, those caring for a parent, child, or spouse, to take leave from employment for up to 12 weeks per year to provide care.

The leave is unpaid (in most states) and it is restricted to those working for companies with 50 or more employees and who have worked for the employer for at least 12 months, for a minimum of 1,250 hours in that period. Upon return, employees are not guaranteed their same position, although they are guaranteed equivalent pay and benefits. State laws may provide more expansive coverage than the FMLA, but the Act establishes minimal federal standards and rights to unpaid leave for employees.

A survey on the impact of the Act found that those worksites that are covered by it have little difficulty in complying and report no negative impacts on profitability and productivity (Abt Associates, 2013). In addition, most employees receive some pay while on leave. The findings also show that women are more likely to take leave; however, they still report a greater unmet need for more leave than men. Expanding the law so that it covers more workers, those working for smaller firms, and those working fewer hours would increase its effectiveness in meeting the right to work for these caregivers.

About 40% of the workforce is not eligible for leave under the FMLA (www.nationalpartnership.org, retrieved July 2014). The restrictions of the Act make it difficult for low-income employees to use their leave as they potentially forfeit their salary and benefits. Those working less than full time, temporary workers, and seasonal workers are not eligible, and the Act also applies only to care provided to a spouse, child, or parent. Same-sex couples living in states that recognize same-sex marriage, as well as those working for the federal government, are covered, while those in domestic partnerships or civil unions are not. Expanding the law to cover these groups would help to assure their ability to continue as employed caregivers by assisting them in balancing the demands of caregiving and employment and would substantiate their right to work.

OLDER PERSONS AS CAREGIVERS: THE ROLE OF GRANDPARENTS

In response to shifts and changes in the structure of families and to changing social conditions, the role of grandparents in American society is being redefined. Overall, approximately 6.3% of all children under the age of 18 are being raised in a grandparent-headed household (U.S. Census Bureau, 2010). Increasingly, grandparents, rather than playing peripheral roles in the lives of their grandchildren, are becoming responsible for raising them. In 2010, about 7% of children in the United States lived in a household headed by a grandparent, and more than half of these grandparents had primary responsibility for most of the child's needs (U.S. Census Bureau, 2010). In almost half of these grandparent-headed households (43%), there was no parent present. When kinship care is discussed, it is primarily referring to grandparents who are the vast majority of the caregivers for children whose parents are not present.

Compared to other households, grandmothers raising grandchildren are more likely to be poor (U.S. Census Bureau, 2010), more likely to be receiving public assistance, and less likely to have health insurance. A large proportion (22%) are African American and one-third of the grandparents report a disability. Children living in kinship care face more socioeconomic risks that can affect their development than other children; these include a greater risk for poverty, living with a caretaker without a high-school degree, living with a caretaker who does not have a spouse, and living in a household with four or more children (Ehrle, Green, & Clark, 2001).

The majority of grandparent-headed households are informal private arrangements with the grandparents having no formal custody or relationship to the grandchild. Frequently, the grandparents have become the caregivers after a crisis in the family, while others have stepped in when the parent has either been unable or unwilling to provide care. Child welfare agencies, concerned with placing the child with a relative, are often the intermediary, placing the child with the grandparent when the parent can no longer provide care (Child Welfare Information Gateway, 2013).

These grandparents face many challenges including having poor psychological health and distress (Musil et al., 2011), poor physical health (Hughes, Waite, LaPierre, & Luo, 2007), financial strains (Baker & Mutchler, 2010), and behavioral and emotional disturbances in the children (Smith & Palmieri, 2007). In comparison with children in the general U.S. population, children being raised by grandparents have a higher prevalence of behavioral and emotional disturbances (Smith & Palmieri, 2007). Yet, policies and services to assist them remain sparse and underfunded, often severely taxing their ability to care.

Policies and Financial Support

The federal government mandates that states give preference to grandparents over other blood relatives when placing a child in foster care. However, the majority of grandparents do not enter the foster care system and thus are ineligible for foster care payments. Recent data indicates that of the 2,485,000 children being raised by grandparents or in kinship care, only about 16% are in the foster care system (Generations United, 2014).

Fourteen states and the District of Columbia have established "kinship care" or "relative caregiver" programs by statute to provide relatives with benefits to help offset the cost of caring for the grandchild. Eligibility and the actual amount of the payment vary by state. In most states offering the benefits, the grandparents must be part of the child welfare system.

However, grandparents meeting the income requirements of Temporary Assistance for Needy Families (TANF) may apply for a family grant that considers the income and assets of the entire family and aims to meet all of their financial needs so that children can be adequately cared for in their homes. However, these grants are limited to 60 months and have work requirements attached to them. Because of these requirements, their applicability to grandparent caregivers is often restricted.

TANF also has a second type of grant; the "Child-Only" grant provides financial support to the children and is based only on the resources of the child. The resources and income of the grandparent are not considered in these grants. With most grandchildren having low incomes, these Child-Only grants could be a key support for these families. However, the amount of these grants tends to be quite low. Payments in 2010 averaged $423 per month for three children (U.S. Government Accounting Office [GAO], 2011). Children with special or exceptional needs do not receive additional funds unless they also receive Social Security Disability.

Grandparents who become a part of the foster care system are eligible for foster care payments that tend to be more generous than the TANF grants under Title IV-E of the Social Security Act. Federal law requires that relative caregivers caring for children under Title IV-E receive the same foster care payments as nonrelative caregivers. Foster care payments increase with the number of children in the family, with states usually offering higher stipends for children with special needs. However, the payments have limited impact on custodial grandparents as the majority are raising the children informally and are not in the foster care system (Generations United, 2014). States may also use local funds to support unlicensed relatives caring for children in foster care.

For grandparents and other kinship caregivers who cannot adopt either because they do not want to terminate the parents' rights or the parents refuse to give up their rights, subsidized guardianship can provide financial support. The program is available in 35 states, with most states linking the subsidies to the payment levels of foster care, TANF, and adoption assistance payments. States vary in their regulations with regard to subsidies, with some mandating background and criminal checks, or that the child has special needs or is below a specific income level. In most states, the program is limited to those who have grandchildren who have been in the foster care system. Federal money is generally not available for guardianship subsidies.

Housing Assistance

Having a suitable place to live can be another challenge for many grandparents. Many may qualify for Section 8 Housing under the Department of Housing and Urban Development (HUD), either through the tenant-based voucher system or the project-based voucher program that offers assistance in a specific building. The Section 8 Family Unification Program gives priority to families that are at risk of losing custody of their grandchildren due to inadequate housing. This program can potentially be very relevant to grandparents, but often they are not perceived as qualifying families and are turned away as ineligible by untrained staff (Generations United, 2005).

Section 202, the Supportive Housing for the Elderly program, funds nonprofit developers to build subsidized rental housing for older persons. Tenants are also given rent subsidies. However, the waiting list for this housing is generally very long. In 2011, just over one-third of persons 62 and older with incomes at or below 50% of the area's median income received 202 housing (National Council of State Housing Agencies [NCSHA], 2014). Eligibility requirements are that the person be at least 62 years of age with an income less than 50% of the area median.

Section 202 housing permits children to reside with otherwise eligible elderly family members. However, the Housing for Older Persons Act allows individual owners of privately owned senior-occupied buildings to exclude children if at least 80% of the units are occupied by persons 55 years or older. This requirement, and the scarcity of the housing, prevent it from being a major housing resource for grandparents and deny children the right to live securely in the community.

Health Care

The transition into and out of caregiving appears to have the most negative impact on grandparents' health. Data from the Health and Retirement Study show those newly involved in caregiving for the children have more health declines than non-caregiver grandparents, including increases in depression (Baker & Silverstein, 2008). In addition, these new caregivers have increased rates of obesity and poorer self-rated health (Hughes, Waite, LaPierre, & Luo, 2007). At the same time, higher rates of depression also occurred when the caregivers stopped raising the grandchild (Baker & Silverstein, 2008).

Grandparent caregivers are also less likely than non-caregivers to have preventive care such as cholesterol screening, Pap tests, and flu vaccinations (Baker & Silverstein, 2008). As the health of grandparent caregivers is generally poorer than their non-caregiving peers, raising grandchildren appears to negatively impact their health (Hughes, Waite, LaPierre, & Luo, 2007; Musil, et al., 2011). Greater access to health services, including health education and promotion programs, and mental health services could benefit this population and help fulfill their rights to health and health care.

SUMMARY

The right of the family, which remains the stalwart factor in the support of older persons, is tacitly but not fully recognized by existing policies. Without such recognition, caregivers who play major roles in maintaining these families face undue discrimination. Only three major federal policies—the Family Support Program under the Older Americans Act, the Lifetime Respite Act, and the FMLA—clearly focus on the roles that families assume in providing care and support. Yet, although they provide recognition, their ability to actually make a difference in the lives of caregivers is severely thwarted by a lack of adequate funding.

Much research has documented the strains and stress of family caregivers. Policies to meet their needs have been enacted but receive little priority with regard to implementation. The Lifetime Respite Act, which can provide vital support for caregivers, bolstering their rights for protection and security, remains seriously underfunded. The FMLA, which supports the right to work, has limited applicability to many groups of caregivers, including those with low income whose own financial sovereignty and future Social Security can be jeopardized by taking the leave.

The rights of grandparent caregivers to have security and protection by society remain at risk. Although policies have been developed to assist them, they also remain underfunded and fragmented, and many continue to struggle to provide for their grandchildren. Appropriate and suitable housing remains a major concern and inaccessible to the majority of grandparents. Both their needs and their right to live securely in the community remain unmet.

Without a full recognition of the rights and policies that support them, caregivers in the United States face discrimination. Although caregiving has become a social issue impacting families across society, it is still treated as an individual family concern, and policies to enable caregivers are given precarious attention. Until it is identified as shared responsibility between families and society, and until caregivers and care receivers continue to have human rights, the positions of each will remain precarious. Fragmentation among policies with inadequate funding and resources will continue to undermine these families.

Family caregivers reflect a strong commitment to values that are fundamental to the cohesiveness and humanity of society. Even those assuming the role out of default, rather than choice, attest to the importance that values have on family care and responsibilities. Assuring that caregivers are able to enact these roles with a minimum of stress and a maximum of rewards should be a common goal of social policy. Such a policy would help sustain the dignity, well-being, and human rights of both caregivers and those receiving care.

QUESTIONS FOR DISCUSSION

1. What are some of the roles played by the family in later life? How do these relate to human rights? Discuss the values and beliefs associated with the family and older adults.

2. Describe some of the challenges experienced by grandparent caregivers.

3. How effective is the FMLA for family caregivers? What are its restrictions? What might make it more effective?

4. What would you do to strengthen family policy in the United States to make it more reflective of human rights?

REFERENCES

Abt Associates. (2013). *Family and medical leave in 2012: Technical report prepared for U.S. Department of Labor.* Cambridge: Author.

Administration on Aging. (2012). *National family caregiver support program* (OAA Title IIIE). Washington, DC: Author.

Administration on Aging. (2013). *AOA program evaluations and related reports.* Washington, DC: Author.

Antonnucci, T., & Depner, C. (1982). Social support and informal helping relationships. In T. A. Willis (Ed.), *Basic processes in helping relationships.* New York: Academic Press.

Antonucci, T., Birditt, K., & Webster, N. (2010). Social relations and mortality: A more nuanced approach. *Journal of Health Psychology, 15*(5), 649–659.

Baker, L., & Silverstein, M. (2008). Preventive health behaviors among grandmothers raising grandchildren. *The Journals of Gerontology, Series B-Psychological Sciences and Social Sciences, 63,* S304–S311.

Baker, L., & Mutchler, J. (2010). Poverty and material hardship in grandparent-headed households. *Journal of Marriage and Family, 72.*

Buhler-Wilkerson, K. (2007). Care of the chronically ill at home: An unresolved dilemma in health policy for the United States. *The Milbank Quarterly, 85*(4), 611–639.

Child Welfare Information Gateway. (2013). *Placement of children with relatives.* Retrieved from https://www.childwelfare.gov/systemwide/laws_policies/statutes/placement.pdf

Colello, K., & Napili, A. (2010). *Older Americans Act: Funding*. Congressional Research Service. Washington, DC: Author.

Ehrle, R., Green, R., & Clark, R. (2001). *Children reared by relatives: How are they faring?* Washington, DC: Urban Institute.

Feinberg, L., Reinhard, S., Houser, A., & Choula, R. (2011). *Valuing the invaluable: 2011 Update-The growing contributions and costs of family caregiving*. AARP Public Policy Institute. Washington, DC: Author.

Freedman, V. (1996). Family structure and nursing home admission. *Journal of Gerontology, Social Sciences, 51B*, S261–S269.

Gaugler, J., Duval, S., Anderson, K., & Kane, R. (2007). *Predicting nursing home admission in the U.S.: A meta-analysis*. Retrieved from http://link.springer.com/article/10.1186%2F1471-2318-7-13/fulltext.html

Gaugler, J., Wall, M., Kane, R., & Menk, J. (2011). Does caregiver burden mediate the effects of behavioral disturbances on nursing home admission? *The American Journal of Geriatric Psychiatry, 19*, 497–506.

Generations United. (2014). *The state of grandfamilies in America*: 2014. Washington, DC: Author.

Giunta, N. (2010). The National Family Caregiver Support Program: A multivariate examination of state-level implementation. *Journal of Aging & Social Policy, 22*, 249–266.

Giselle, K., & Cruess, D. (2011). The impact of familism on physical and mental health among Hispanics in the Giselle United States. *Health Psychology Review, 8*, 95–127.

Ho, S., Chan, A., Woo, J., Chong, P., & Sham, A. (2009). Impact of caregiving on health and quality of life: A population-based study of caregivers for elderly persons and non-caregivers. *Journal of Gerontology, Series A: Biological & Medical Sciences, 63*, 873–879.

Houser, A., Gibson, M., & Redfoot, D. (2010). *Trends in family caregiving and paid home care for older people with disabilities in the community: Data from the National Long-Term Care Survey*. Washington, DC: AARP Public Policy Institute.

Hughes, M., Waite, L., LaPierre, T., & Luo, Y. (2007). All in the family: The impact of caring for grandchildren on grandparents health. *Journal of Gerontology, Series B: Psychological Sciences and Social Sciences, 62*, S108–S119.

Koerin, B., Harrigan, M., & Secret, M. (2008). Eldercare and employed caregivers: A public private responsibility. *Journal of Gerontological, Social Work, 51*(1–2), 143–161.

Lahale, C., Earle, A., & Heymann, J. (2013). An uneven burden: Social disparities in adult caregiving responsibilities, working conditions, and caregiver outcomes. *Research on Aging, 35*, 243–274.

Lim, W., Cheah, W., Noorhazlina, A., & Han, H. (2014). Worry about performance: A unique dimension of caregiver burden. *International Geriatrics, 26,* 677–686.

Litwak, E. (1985). Helping the Elderly, The Complementary Roles of informal networks and formal systems. New York, Guilford.

Lyons, K., Zarit, S., Sayer, C., & Whitlatch, C. (2002). Caregiving as a dyadic process. *Journal of Gerontology, Psychological Sciences and Social Sciences, 57,* 195–204.

Musil, C., Gordon, N., Warner, C., Zauszniewski, J., Standing, T., & Wykle, M. (2011). Grandmothers and caregiving to grandchildren: Continuity, change, and outcomes over 24 months. *The Gerontologist, 51,* 86–100.

Napili, A., & Colello, K. (2013). *Funding for the Older Americans Act and Other Aging Services Programs.* Congressional Research Service. Washington, DC.

National Alliance for Caregiving (NAC) and AARP. (2009). *Caregiving in the U.S.* Bethesda, MD: NAC, and Washington, DC: AARP. Funded by the MetLife Foundation.

National Council of State Housing Agencies. (2014). *Harvard's Joint Center for Housing Studies Releases Report on Housing America's older adults.* Retrieved from https://www.ncsha.org/blog/harvard%E2%80%99s-joint-center-housing-studies-releases-report-housing-america%E2%80%99s-older-adults

Pew Research Center. (2010). *Social and demographic trends: The decline of marriage and rise of new families.* Washington, DC: Author.

Pillemer, K., & Suitor, J. J. (2006). Making choices: A within-family study of caregiver selection. *The Gerontologist, 46,* 439–448.

Pinquart, M., & Sörensen, S. (2006). Gender differences, caregiver stressors, social resources, and health: An updated meta-analysis. *Journal of Gerontology, Series B: Psychological Sciences and Social Sciences, 61,* 33–45.

Pope, N., Kolomer, S., & Glass, G. (2012). How women in late midlife become caregivers for their aging parents. *Journal of Women and Aging, 24,* 242–261.

Radina, M. E. (2007). Mexican American siblings caring for aging parents: Processes of caregiver selection designation. *Journal of Comparative Family Studies, 38,* 143–163.

Roth, D., Perkins, M., Wadlety, V., Temple, E., & Haley, W. (2009). Family caregiving and emotional strain: Associations with quality of life in a large national sample of middle-aged and older adults. *Quality of Life Research, 18,* 679–688.

Savundranqyagam, M., Hummert, M., Montgomery, R., & Braun, D. (2005). Investigating the effects of communication problems on caregiver burden. *Journal of Gerontology Series B: Psychology and Social Sciences, 60,* S48–S55.

Scharlach, A., Dal Santo, T., Lehning, A., Gustavson, K., Lee, S., Auh, E., et al. (2006). *Caregiving in California: Final report of the University of California family caregiver support project*. Berkeley, CA: Center for the Advanced Study of Aging Service.

Smith, G., & Palmieri, P. (2007). Risk of psychological difficulties among children raised by custodial grandparents. *Psychiatric Services, 58*, 1303–1310.

Spillman, B., & Long, S. (2009). Does high caregiver stress predict nursing home entry? *Inquiry, 46*, 140–161.

U.S. Census Bureau, American Community Survey. (2010). *1-Year Estimates: table S1001 and 2005: table B10001*. Accessed at http://factfinder2.census.gov, on March 7, 2012.

U.S. Government Accounting Office (GAO). (2011). *TANF and Child Welfare Programs: Increased data could improve access to benefits and services*. Washington, DC: GAO.

CHAPTER 8

The Most Vulnerable Groups of Older Adults

As long as chronological age is permitted to serve as a defining measure of one's worth, older adults remain a vulnerable population. However, within the population of older adults, vulnerability is not uniform as specific subgroups are more likely to be at risk of discrimination, which jeopardizes their very basic human rights: security, liberty, dignity, employment, and having an adequate standard of living. In its most extreme form, this vulnerability can result in elder abuse in which not only the rights but also the safety and even lives of older adults are in jeopardy.

WOMEN

Discrimination against women is a global phenomenon. The Convention on the Elimination of All Forms of Discrimination Against Women (CEDAW), which came into effect in 1998, was approved by 170 countries but has still not been ratified by the United States. The intent of the convention was to ensure that women's equal rights are equivalent to those of men. In 1995, the Fourth World Conference on Women adopted the Beijing Declaration and Platform for Action with the goals of developing equality and peace for women, requesting that all governments take necessary steps to counter discrimination, and promoting equality and freedom for women throughout the life cycle (United Nations, 1995). Unfortunately, this declaration also remains to be implemented. The inequality that women face throughout their life span makes them particularly vulnerable to having rights ignored in their later years.

Within the United States, women continue to outlive men with an average life expectancy at birth of 79.4 years compared to that of men, which is 73.9 years. They also live an average of 15–20 years as widows. In addition to being more likely to be living alone, older women are nearly twice as likely as older men to be poor (Women's National Law Center, 2014). The low-paying jobs that they often have are usually without benefits or pensions, causing them to rely on Social Security as a sole source of income. However, their average payments are $4,500 less than those of men (Women's National Law Center, 2014). In 2011, the average income for a woman over 65 was $14,000, compared to $24,300 for a man (Wider Opportunities for Women, 2012). About 60% of women over 65 do not have sufficient income to cover basic living expenses as compared to 41% of men in the same age group (Wider Opportunities for Women, 2012).

Long-term care is a significant burden for older women, as they are more likely than men to be both caregivers and care receivers. The majority of caregivers (61%) are women and most are middle-aged, with more than 13% being 65 years and older (Office on Women's Health, 2014). Because women outlive men, they are more likely to be living alone. Their longer life spans also mean that they are more likely to develop chronic illnesses and impairments that can impede their functioning and cause them to become "care receivers" (Kaiser Family Foundation, 2013). Moreover, they are more likely to need formal support services in order to remain in the community and are also more likely to live in nursing homes, assisted living, and other long-term care institutions (Kaiser Family Foundation, 2013).

However, older women are often reluctant to relocate, desiring to age in place (Center for Housing Policy, 2012). Moreover, most older women are unable to afford the costs of long-term care facilities, including assisted living, which averages approximately $87,000 annually (Scan Foundation, 2013). Consequently, many remain at risk of isolation and in need of support in the community.

Medicare plays an important role in the lives of older women who comprise more than half (56%) of all beneficiaries. But the limitations that Medicare presents with regard to long-term care coverage is that many women face very high out-of-pocket spending with the amount escalating for those over age 85 (Kaiser Family Foundation, 2013). Data from 2009 show that the annual income of 60% of women age 85 and over was $20,000, with out-of-pocket medical spending of $7,555 (Kaiser Family Foundation, 2013).

Medicaid is an important resource for women across the life span, and is particularly important for women over 65, who comprise 69% of the recipients in this age group (National Women's Law Center, 2012). Moreover, 25% of women over age 85 on Medicare are also on Medicaid and, in addition to being poor, have worse health status and more health needs than those only on Medicare (Kaiser Family Foundation, 2013). The role of Medicaid in the support of older women is further underscored by the fact that 62% of all older women in nursing homes are covered by both Medicaid and Medicare (Kaiser Family Foundation, 2013).

Consequently, the security and health care of older women remains a subject of major concern. The experiences of women throughout their life span differ from those of men with regard to employment and income, making them more vulnerable to financial insecurity and poverty as they age. They are also at increased risk of being without support, which could enable them to remain in the community when they need assistance. Without policies that recognize the barriers that they face throughout the life span, their rights as older adults remain in jeopardy.

LESBIAN, GAY, BISEXUAL, AND TRANSGENDER ELDERS

There is no clear estimate of the number of older lesbian, gay, bisexual, and transgender elders (LGBT) in the United States. Data from the American Community Survey estimate that the number of same-sex couples over the age of 65 has grown from 4.9% in 2005 to 6.3% in 2011 (Gates, 2013). Further estimates suggest that there are 1.5–7 million older adults who are LGBT and that this number will double by 2030 (Fitzgerald, 2013). The sexual orientations and identities of these older adults coupled with age discrimination increases their risk of vulner-ability and having their rights violated.

LGBT adults are more likely to be poor than their heterosexual peers, and this scenario is more likely to be common among lesbian couples (Badgett, Durso, & Schneebaum, 2013). Discrimination throughout the lifetime and a lack of access to benefits may partially account for their lower incomes. Their increased risk of poverty may also result from the greater likelihood that they will be living alone, which means that their household incomes are lower than that of other seniors.

Data from a national study of over 2,500 older LGBT adults found that in comparison to heterosexuals, LGBT elders have higher rates of disability and mental distress, and are more likely to smoke or indulge in excessive drinking (Fredriksen-Goldsen et al., 2013). Lesbian and bisexual older women have a higher risk of cardiovascular disease and obesity than heterosexual women, while older gay and bisexual men are more likely to have poor physical health than their heterosex-ual peers (Fredriksen-Goldsen et al., 2013).

The LGBT older population is at increased risk of isolation as they are less likely to be married or in a relationship with a partner; hence, they are more likely to be living alone than their heterosexual peers. When they need assistance with caregiving, they are more likely to rely on assistance from friends, the family of choice, rather than their own family (Muraco, Fredriksen, & Goldsen, 2011). In addition, these caregivers tend to be of similar age to the care receiver, suggesting that they may not be able to provide all of the care that their partner requires. As these caregivers are often not covered by employer benefit plans, and the federal Family and Medical Leave Act (FMLA) does not require that employers provide them with leave to care for a same-sex partner or spouse, they are at risk of strug-gling to balance caregiving with work.

Long-Term Care

The majority of long-term care services in the United States are pro-vided informally by the family. This places an untold burden on LGBT elders, who have higher poverty rates than older heterosexuals and are twice as likely to be single and three to four times more likely to be without relatives to provide care (SAGE, 2014). This isolation can be a further obstacle to care, as often they have no one to help them navigate the web of long-term care services.

The Medicaid spousal impoverishment protections that were established in 1988 to protect the spouse of a person in a nursing home from losing their home and assets do not require that states treat same-sex couples in the same way. Consequently, those living in states that do not recognize their relationship are unlikely to be eligible and partners of those in an institution are left financially vulnerable in the community.

Nursing homes and other types of institutional care present further problems for this population. A survey of 769 older LGBT adults found that the majority believed that staff of long-term care facilities would discriminate against them if they were open about their sexual orientation (Lamda legal, 2011). A majority of the respondents also reported experiencing staff harassment and mistreatment on the basis of their sexual orientation, claiming their rights were ignored (Lamda Legal, 2011).

Policy Changes

Since the Supreme Court declared the Defense of Marriage Act (DOMA) unconstitutional in June 2013, Social Security began processing widows' and widowers' claims to survivor benefits in legally recognized same-sex marriages. With the defeat of DOMA, the Internal Revenue Service (IRS) is also reframing its system to provide greater tax equity for married same-sex couples with regard to flexible savings accounts and flexible spending accounts, permitting the same-sex spouse and dependents to be covered and reimbursed in the same way as heterosexual spouses.

Medicare benefits continue to be based on the individual. Same-sex married couples do not receive the same benefit as that of other married couples; that is, a spouse is permitted to be covered by Medicare if the other spouse is covered. In addition, legally married same-sex couples who live in states that do not recognize their marriage will not be able to access the spousal benefits available to heterosexual couples. However, all married couples are entitled to the same coverage in nursing homes.

Without policies that are responsive to the specific needs of older LGBT adults, their rights continue to be violated. Ensuring that federal and state programs, such as Social Security, Medicaid, Supplemental Security Income (SSI), and Social Security Disability Insurance (SSDI), include benefits for partners could provide them with increased financial security. Recognition by FMLA of the role that their caregivers play could provide further support for partners providing assistance. Finally, the staff of programs for older adults needs to be sensitized to the needs of this population to ensure that persons feel comfortable and accepted in their facilities and services.

The LGBT Elder Americans Act was introduced into the Senate in September 2012 (S.3575) and has not moved out of committee. The Act would increase federal funding to organizations serving these older adults and their caregivers, collect data on discrimination, include LGBT older adults as a vulnerable population with the greatest economic and social needs under the Older Americans Act (OAA), prioritize research and development grants for organizations to facilitate access to services, and improve LGBT health care and long-term care needs.

In 2010, the Administration on Aging (AOA) established the LGBT aging center (lgbtagingcenter.org). The center offers technical assistance to agencies and programs with regard to health and social issues faced by these seniors. Specifically, the resource center is intended to educate organizations dealing with aging on the special needs of LGBT elders, sensitize LGBT organizations about the existence and special needs of older adults, and educate LGBT individuals about the need to plan ahead for long-term care.

OLDER IMMIGRANTS

Between 1990 and 2010, the number of immigrants in the United States over the age of 65 almost doubled from 2.7 million to nearly 5 million (Leach, 2008–2009). They now comprise 12% of all immigrants in the country, a proportion similar to that of the general population over 65 years (Migration Policy Institute, 2012). Seventy-three percent of all older immigrants are naturalized citizens.

One out of seven older immigrants was born in Mexico and, not surprisingly, the most common language spoken by the population is Spanish. The longer people have been in the United States, the more likely they are to speak English. Those less skilled in English will depend more on the family (Wilmoth, 2012).

Compared to their native born peers, 40% of older immigrants are more likely to be living in poverty, as compared to 30% of other older adults, with half of them having less than $11,000 in individual income per year (Migration Policy Institute). Moreover, the gap in income between that of older immigrants and native born is expected to increase, as these immigrants tend to have less marketable skills (Borjas, 2013).

Older immigrants tend to live with their relatives, particularly if the child is the sponsor (Wilmoth, 2012). With limited knowledge of English, they are often reluctant to use public transportation on their own and are at greater risk of becoming isolated. This risk often contributes to depression and stress as acculturation levels, and thus expectations, within the family can significantly vary (Treas, 2009).

Access to Public Benefits

Immigrant older adults receive public assistance at more than twice the rate as those born in the United States (Borjas, 2013). Most of this assistance is through SSI; however, as with other federal benefits, this assistance is only for those who are naturalized citizens or for those who entered the United States before 1996. Those entering after 1996 and who are not citizens are barred from receiving federal benefits.

The restrictions of Medicare and Medicaid impact the health care of many older immigrants. Medicare Part A benefits are available to immigrants who have become citizens and have worked in the United States for 10 years. Immigrants who have been permanent residents for 5 years are able to buy Medicare from the government. Medicaid maintains the 5-year residency requirement for eligibility, although many states ignore the rule and offer coverage. The 5-year rule also pertains to the Affordable Care Act (ACA), which provides coverage to older legal residents who have lived in the United States for at least 5 years.

States have the administrative authority to make many decisions regarding eligibility for benefit programs for noncitizens and thus there remains great variability with regard to access. Most legal immigrants who are permanent residents are able to get food stamps (SNAP). Between 2006 and 2010, 20% of elderly Hispanic immigrants were receiving food stamps, in comparison to 5% of those elderly born in the United States (Gerst & Burr, 2012).

The restrictions of benefits mean that many are being denied access to services, even though they are legal residents of the United States. With regard to health, these restrictions mean that many who are in need of preventive health care and treatment are unable to obtain services, placing them at further risk. This lack of access for older immigrants severely impacts their human rights as they are denied services that are critical for their health and well-being.

MINORITIES

The population of the United States is both racially and ethnically diverse, and this diversity is reflected among older adults. In the general population who are 65 and older, 8.5% are Black, 6.8% are Hispanic, and 3.3% are Asian, with the Hispanic elderly increasing most rapidly (U.S. Census Bureau, 2012). Racial and ethnic minorities accounted for 19% of the older population but 36% of the elderly poor, with the highest poverty rates among older Hispanic women (38.8%) and older Black women (32.2%) who live alone (U.S. Census Bureau, 2012).

Social Security comprises 90% of the income for one-third of older African Americans and Hispanics, with about one quarter of older African Americans and Hispanics depending on it for all of their income, in comparison to 14% of older Whites (Waid, Koening, & Caldera, 2012). In comparison to older Whites who have a median SSI of $19,575, minorities receive significantly less. The median income for older African Americans and Hispanics is $14,400 and for Asians, $17,957 (Waid & Caldera, 2012). Lifetimes of lower earning, higher rates of disability, and less access to pensions and retirement plans contribute to their reduced incomes and higher rates of poverty.

Chronic health conditions that impact the quality of life of older adults also vary by race and ethnicity. Data from the Health Interview Survey show non-Hispanic Blacks to have higher levels of hypertension (69% compared to 54%) and diabetes (32% compared to 18%) than non-Hispanic Whites, as well as more difficulty with physical functioning (Liao et al., 2011). Non-Hispanic Whites are also more likely than Black or Hispanic older adults to report their health as either excellent or good.

However, there are variations among the many Hispanic groups in the United States. Puerto Ricans, the second largest Hispanic subgroup in the United States, report having the poorest health status and the highest prevalence of many acute and chronic illnesses when compared to non-Hispanic older adults and other Hispanic groups (Tucker et al., 2010). Data indicate that 21% of older Puerto Ricans, in comparison to 15% of Cuban and Mexican Americans, report some activity limitation (Hajat, Lucas, & Kington, 2000).

The older Asian population also varies with regard to indicators of health status. Vietnamese and Filipinos have the highest rates of asthma, hypertension, and heart disease. Korean older adults report the fewest chronic diseases, but also report the most distress, while the lowest levels of distress are found among Japanese (Kim et al., 2010). The majority of older Japanese (59%) and Filipinos (54%) rate their health as excellent or very good, while nearly half (45%) of Vietnamese rate their health as poor. Such variations have been associated with the ability to speak English well, as well as different immigration patterns and length of time in the United States.

Medicare is particularly important for minority older adults and yet, with their very low incomes and assets, they often have difficulty with the co-pays and deductibles. In 2010, Medicare beneficiaries spent nearly 15% of their household incomes on health care (Families USA, 2013), which poses a large strain on those with limited finances. As a result of the cost of care, many minority elderly delay seeking needed health services (Cubanski & Dulio, 2011). Difficulties in access to care mean less monitoring and screening, less timely diagnoses, and less treatment of chronic illnesses.

Poverty and poor health status contribute to the role that Medicaid plays in the lives of older minority adults. Within the Medicaid program, minority elderly comprise 43% of its participants (NAACP, 2014).

Consequently, any changes or reductions in the program that might restrict its benefits would put the health and health care of these adults at undue risk.

Long-Term Care

Minority elderly share with others the desire to remain in their homes in the community as long as possible. Most prefer informal care to formal care; however, with changes in the availability of traditional caregivers, this preference can become more difficult to fulfill. Consequently, formal home and community services may be needed to provide support as needs increase. Those above the Medicaid eligibility guidelines are most at risk as they are unlikely to have sufficient funds to pay for services. In fact, disparities in access to home- and community-based services (HCBS) are believed to have contributed to the rapid increase of minorities, between 1999 and 2008, in nursing homes (Feng, Fennell, Typer, Clark, & Mor, 2011). With an absence of caregivers and less access to community services, nursing homes become the only option for care.

HCBS continue to be underused by minority older adults and their caregivers. Problems in accessing services, difficulties with language, and the fragmentation of programs continue to contribute to underutilization of community-based long-term care services (Scharlach, Kellam, Ong, Baskin, Goldstein, & Fox, 2006). In addition, previous negative experiences with formal services and an overall distrust of them can further deter utilization. Research on the use of Title III services by older Hispanics, African Americans, and Whites found that Hispanics had the highest rate of unmet hours of care and African Americans were more likely to enter a nursing home when they needed assistance (Herrera, 2013).

Unfortunately, the quality of nursing homes serving minorities is likely to be poor with more deficiencies than those serving Whites (Smith, Feng, Fennell, Zinn, & Mor, 2007). A study of Hispanics 65 and over in nursing homes found a greater likelihood of Hispanics living in poorer quality nursing homes than non-Hispanic peers with deficiencies associated with staffing, the use of restraints, inspections, and financial viability of the homes (Fennell, Feng, Clark, & Mor,

2010). Consequently, even when persons make the decision to use a nursing home, they must continue to be concerned about the care that they receive and how it fulfills their human rights.

ELDER ABUSE

Vulnerability itself can be a precursor to the most extreme violation of human rights, elder abuse. As victims, older adults are robbed of their humanity, being denied security, protection, and dignity, and often the right to life itself. Elder abuse refers to abuse, neglect, and exploitation, including any known, intentional, or negligent act by a caregiver or any other person that causes harm or serious risk of harm to a vulnerable adult (AOA, 2013). The abuse can be physical, sexual, neglect, exploitation, emotional, abandonment, or self-neglect.

Increasingly, during the past few years attention has been given to elder abuse but, at the same time, it has become a catch-all term for various wrongs against older people (Anetzberger, 2012). For many years, abuse was viewed as the outcome of caregiver stress, with stress being a predictor of maltreatment. However, stress is almost a normal part of caregiving and most caregivers do not harm the care receiver. In fact, the most harmful outcomes of stress associated with caregiving are those afflicting the caregiver, such as anxiety, substance abuse, overeating, depression, and social isolation (Hoffman & Mendez-Luck, 2011).

Risk factors for abuse include a lack of social support for the victim, social isolation of both the victim and the abuse perpetrator, substance abuse by the perpetrator, behavior problems of the perpetrator or the victim, and poor or declining physical and mental health of the victim (Anetzberger, 2012). Financial exploitation has been associated with low income of the victims, physical disability, poor health, and low social support. Physical, emotional, neglect, and sexual abuse have been associated with unemployed perpetrators, as well as substance abusers and those with mental problems (Acierno, 2010).

The consequences of abuse are due to an increase in mortality for those with self-neglect and for those subjected to physical and verbal abuse (Dong, 2009). The financial costs of abuse to victims were estimated at $2.9 billion in 2011 (MetLife Mature Market Institute, 2011). Even those assigned to protect older adults may be perpetrators. Guardians appointed by courts took $5.4 million in assets from their older wards in 2009 (U.S. Government Accounting Office, 2010).

The federal government has responded to the problem of elder abuse through the establishment of the National Center on Elder Abuse (NCEA), Title II of the OAA, in 1988. It acts as a resource center to states and local agencies by providing information and technical assistance. In 2011, the NCEA awarded grants for elder abuse prevention in Indian Country and for the development of the NCEA Information Clearinghouse. However, its ability to make any real impact on elder abuse is constricted due to limited funding. Moreover, there is no consensus among states as to what constitutes abuse, meaning that it may or may not be seen as a legal issue (Anetzberger, 2012). Additionally, as long as abuse is perceived as a family problem, there is a propensity to respond through forms of individual treatment and interventions rather than through social policies that protect vulnerable older adults (Brandl & Raymond, 2012).

The Elder Justice Act (EJA) was enacted in 2010 as part of the Patient Protection and Affordable Care Act. It establishes a Coordinating Council that will make recommendations to the Secretary of Health and Human Services on the coordination of agencies related to elder abuse, neglect, and exploitation. It has allotted $400 million over 4 years to Adult Protective Services, has allotted $100 million for state demonstration projects, and provides grants for establishing forensic centers, long-term care ombudsman training, and training of staff in long-term care facilities. To date, no money has actually been appropriated to the Act even though it was passed with bipartisan support.

In 2012, The Elder Protection and Abuse Prevention Act was introduced into the Senate. This Act would help strengthen federal resources for states to assist them in preventing and responding to cases of elder abuse. The Act would refine the definition of abuse, neglect, and elder justice and define financial exploitation and adult protective services. It would also require all states to incorporate standardized elder abuse screening and reporting protocols. Though most states currently have mandatory reporting laws, cases are still missed due to a lack of integrated screening. The Act that would assist state Adult Protective Services by helping them to incorporate screenings into their senior programs remains in committee in Congress.

The Elder Abuse Victims Act of 2013 would establish an Office of Elder Justice within the Department of Justice that would provide information, training, and technical assistance to states and local governments to prevent, investigate, and prosecute the impact of abuse and its physical and psychological outcomes; evaluate ways to address and respond to abuse; evaluate training models to investigate abuse; and study state laws and practices related to abuse. However, as with the 2012 Bill, this proposed legislation also remains in committee.

SUMMARY

Vulnerability places older adults at grave risk of having many of their human rights violated. These are persons who have faced discrimination throughout their lives, and if they become dependent with age they are bound to face increasing inequalities. The rights to full participation in society, the rights to a decent income, and the rights to appropriate health care are among the key rights that remain most at risk for many in these groups of older adults. Although needs have been well researched and documented, policies that address them and assure that duty bearers fulfill them as human rights have yet to be fully supported.

With poverty being a common concern, assuring that programs offer income protection is fundamental to fulfilling their human rights. Social Security plays a dominant role in the income of these older adults. As it is based upon earnings, those with years of low wages are destined to face retirement with less financial security. In addition, those most dependent upon it are also the least likely to have private pensions to rely on.

Health and long-term care are also major concerns that can jeopardize human rights. Particularly vulnerable are those who are not eligible for Medicaid but do not have the resources to pay for the needed services. Expanding Medicaid so that it reaches more people and provides older adults with more resources could increase the accessibility of community services and permit many to remain in the community. Increasing outreach, and having providers fluent in the older adult's language and sensitive to their cultures, may also help sustain them in the community.

Responding to the needs of older women and addressing their rights must begin much earlier in the life span. The inequalities faced by older women are a product of years of discrimination. Their risk of poverty results from lifetimes of lower earnings, more interrupted work histories, and fewer employer benefits. With low Social Security benefits, the main source of income for most older women is further compromised. Every alteration that limits income, benefits, and health care for this population has serious repercussions on their well-being and human rights. The low incomes of older women mean that they are likely to become dependent on Medicaid for either community or institutional care. Thus, any curtailment of Medicaid services is likely to further threaten their health and ability to remain in the community (Families USA, 2011).

LGBT seniors continue to face many challenges as they age. Primary among these is equal access to benefits and services that are mandated for their heterosexual peers. Until such discrimination is overcome, they remain vulnerable to having their rights ignored. At the same time, these rights are becoming recognized at the federal level through the center established in 2010 by the AOA and the Act in Congress that would focus on their needs and rights. Both measures indicate that the population is becoming more visible and that they may begin to experience less discrimination and more equity as policies and programs begin to change.

Owing to their high levels of poverty, a primary necessity for older immigrants is to improve their access to benefit programs. The strict eligibility criteria, based on citizenship and residency requirements, mean that the many who have worked and contributed to the economy are denied federal benefits such as SSI and Medicare, which are available to others. Denying these benefits contributes to poverty and undermines their health status. Both the needs and rights of immigrant older adults are threatened through their ineligibility for these programs.

Many minority elders suffer from poverty and poor health status, and are dependent upon public benefits for their support. Changes in programs such as Social Security, Medicare, and Medicaid that could curtail benefits would further endanger their well-being and rights for protection and security. Their continued underutilization of community services means that the well-being and ability of many to remain in the community is at risk, with many in need of assistance to find the only alternative—a nursing home. Outreach and the expansion of community care to these populations are critical to expanding access and increasing their options for services and supports. Improving the quality of nursing homes is essential to assure that minority residents receive appropriate and proper, rather than substandard, care.

Finally, the issue of elder abuse, although having received much attention, is still impacted by an absence of comprehensive policies and programs. The many legislative bills to deal with this serious problem remain in limbo in Congress. Obtaining adequate funding for existing services is still a problem; thus, many vulnerable adults are subject to becoming victims. Without greater resources and making the issue of abuse a national priority, the rights and even lives of these older adults continue to be at risk.

QUESTIONS FOR DISCUSSION

1. How are the rights of LGBT older adults threatened? What policy changes are needed to protect their rights?

2. How are the rights of immigrant older adults threatened? What policy changes are needed to protect their rights?

3. How do policies impact the rights of older minority persons? What policy changes are needed to protect their rights?

4. Describe the types of elder abuse. What policy changes are needed to protect the rights of older adults who are at risk of abuse?

REFERENCES

Acierno, R. (2010). Prevalence and correlates of emotional, physical, sexual, and financial abuse and potential neglect in the United States: The National Elder Mistreatment Study. *American Journal of Public Health, 100*(2), 292–297.

Administration on Aging (AOA). (2013). *What is elder abuse?* Retrieved from http://www.aoa.gov/AoA_programs/elder_rights/EA_prevention/whatisEA.aspx

Anetzberger, G. (2012). An update on the nature and scope of elder abuse. *Generations, 36,* 12–20.

Badgett, M., Durso, L., & Schneebaum, A. (2013). *New patterns of poverty in the lesbian, gay and bisexual community.* UCLA: The Williams Institute.

Borjas, G. (2013). *The slowdown in the economic assimilation of immigrants.* NBER Working Paper No. 19116.

Brandl, B., & Raymond, J. (2012). Policy implications of recognizing that caregiver stress in not the primary cause of elder abuse. *Generations, 36,* 32–39.

Center for Housing Policy. (2012). *Housing an aging population: Are we prepared?* Washington, DC: Author.

Cubanski, J., & Dulio, A. (2011). *Living close to the edge: Financial challenges and tradeoffs for people on Medicare.* Washington, DC: The Kaiser Family Foundation.

Dong, X. (2009). Elder self-neglect and abuse and mortality risk in a community-dwelling population. *The Journal of the American Medical Association, 302,* 517–526.

Families USA. (2011). *Cutting Medicaid: Harming seniors and people with disabilities who need long-term care.* Retrieved from http://familiesusa.org/sites/default/files/product_documents/Cutting-Medicaid.pdf

Families USA. (2013). *Low income Medicare beneficiaries need better protection from health care costs.* Fact Sheet. Retrieved from www.familiesusa.org/.../fact.../factsheet-medicare-low-income.html

Feng, Z., Fennell, M., Typer, D., Clark, M., & Mor, V. (2011). Growth of racial and ethnic minorities in US nursing homes driven by demographics and possible disparities in options. *Health Affairs, 30,* 1358–1365.

Fennell, M., Feng, A., Clark, M., & Mor, B. (2010). Elderly Hispanics more likely to reside in poor-quality nursing homes. *Health Affairs, 29,* 65–73.

Fitzgerald, E. (2013). *No golden years at the end of the rainbow: How a lifetime of discrimination compounds economic and wealth disparities for LGBT older adults.* Washington, DC: The National Gay and Lesbian Task Force.

Fredriksen-Goldsen, K. I., Kim, H.-J., Barkan, S. E., Muraco, A., & Hoy-Ellis, C. P. (2013). Health disparities among lesbian, gay, and bisexual older adults – Results from a population-based study. *American Journal of Public Health.* Advance online publication. doi:10.2105/AJPH.2012.301110

Gates, J. (2013). *Same-sex and different-sex couples in the American community survey: 2005-2011* (Los Angeles). Retrieved from http://williamsinstitute.law.ucla.edu/wp-content/uploads/ACS-2013.pdf

Gerst, K., & Burr, C. (2012). Welfare program participation among older immigrants. *Public Policy & Aging Report, 22*(2), 12–16.

Hajat, A., Lucas, J. B., & Kington, R. (2000). Health outcomes among Hispanic subgroups: Data from the National Health Interview Survey, 1992–95. *Advances in Data analysis and Classification, 310,* 1–14.

150

Herrera, A. (2013). Caregiver service use, unmet hours of care and independence among Hispanics, African American and Whites. *Home Health Care Services Quarterly, 32,* 35–56.

Hoffman, G., & Mendez-Luck, C. (2011). Stressed and strapped: Caregivers in California. Health Policy Brief for the Center for Health Policy Research. Los Angeles, CA: University of California.

Kaiser Family Foundation. (2013). *Medicare's role for older women.* Issue Brief. Kaiser Family Foundation.

Kim, G., Chiriboga, D. A., Jang, Y., Lee, S., Huang, C.- H., & Parmelee, P. (2010). Health status of older Asian American in California. *Journal of the American Geriatrics Society, 58,* 2003–2008.

Lamda Legal. (2011). *LGBT elders raise serious fears about long term care.* Retrieved from www.lambdalegal.org/.../dc_20110405_lgbt-elders-raise-serious

Leach, M. (2008–2009). America's older immigrants: A profile, generations. *Journal of the American Geriatrics Society, 32*(4), 34–39.

Liao, Y., Bang, D., Cosgrove, S., Dulin, R., Harris, Z., Taylor, A., White, S., Yatabe, G., Liburd, L., Giles, W. (2011). *Surveillance of health status in minority communities - Racial and Ethnic Approaches to Community Health Across the U.S. (REACH U.S.)* Risk Factor Survey, United States, 2009. Division of Adult and Community Health, National Center for Chronic Disease Prevention and Health Promotion; Centers for Disease Control and Prevention (CDC).

MetLife Mature Market Institute. (2011). *The MetLife study of elder financial abuse: Crimes of occasion, desperation, and predation against America's elders.* New York: Metropolitan Life Insurance Company.

Migration Policy Institute. (2012). *Pyramids of U.S. immigrant and native-born populations, 1970-present.* Retrieved from http://www.migrationpolicy.org/programs/data-hub/us-immigration-trends#agesex

Muraco, A., Fredriksen, K., & Goldsen, K. (2011). "That's what friends do": Informal caregiving for chronically ill lesbian, gay, and bisexual elders. *Journal of Social and Personal Relationships, 28,* 1073–1092.

NAACP. (2014). *NAACP strongly opposes draconian cuts to Medicaid program.* Retrieved from http://www.naacp.org/action-alerts/entry/naacp-strongly-opposes-draconian-cuts-to-medicaid-program

National Women's Law Center. (2012). *What the Medicaid eligibility expansion means for women.* Retrieved from http://www.nwlc.org/resource/what-medicaid-eligibility-expansion-means-women

Office on Women's Health, U.S. Department of Health and Human Services. (2014). *Caregiver stress.* Fact Sheet. Retrieved from http://www.womenshealth.gov/publications/our-publications/fact-sheet/caregiver-stress.html

SAGE. (2014). *Out and visible: The experiences of lesbian, gay, bisexual and transgender older adults,* AGes 45–75, New York, Author.

Scan Foundation. (2013). *Overview of current long-term care financing options.* Retrieved from http://thescanfoundation.org/overview-current-long-term-care-financing-options

Scharlach, E., Kellam, R., Ong, N., Baskin, A., Goldstein, C., & Fox, R. (2006). Cultural attitudes and caregiver service use: Lessons from focus groups with racially and ethnically diverse family caregivers. *Journal of Gerontological Social Work, 47,* 133–156.

Smith, D., Feng, Z., Fennell, M., Zinn, J., & Mor, V. (2007). Separate and unequal: Racial segregation and disparities in quality across U.S. Nursing homes. *Health Affairs, 26,* 1448–1458.

Treas, J. (2009). Four myths about older adults in America's immigrant families. *Generations, 32,* 40–45.

Tucker, K., Mattei, J., Noel, S., Collado, B., Mendez, J., Nelson, J. … Falcon, F. (2010). The Boston Puerto Rican Health Study, a longitudinal cohort study on health disparities in Puerto Rican adults: Challenges and opportunities. *BMC Public Health, 10.* Retrieved from http://www.biomedcentral.com/1471-2458/10/107

United Nations. (1995). *Beijing Declaration and platform for action.* Geneva: Author.

U.S. Census Bureau. (2012). *Current population survey, annual social and economic supplement.* Washington, DC: Author.

U.S. Government Accountability Office. (2010). *Guardianships: Cases of financial exploitation, neglect, and abuse of seniors report to the Chairman. Special Committee on Aging.* U.S. Senate. GAO-10-1046. Washington, DC: Government Printing Office.

Waid, M., Koening, G., & Caldera, S. (2012). *Older Americans: Key indicators of well-being chart book.* AARP Public Policy Institute. Washington, DC: AARP.

Wilmoth, J. (2012). A demographic profile of older immigrants. *Public Policy and Aging Report, 22,* 8–11.

Wider Opportunities for Women. (2013). *Living below the line: Economic insecurity and older Americans.* Retrieved from http://www.wowonline.org/wp-content/uploads/2013/09/Living-Below-the-Line-Economic-Insecurity-and-Older-Americans-Women-Sept-2013.pdf

Women's National Law Center. (2014). *Women and Social Security.* Retrieved from http://www.nwlc.org/resource/women-and-social-security

CHAPTER 9

Global Aging, Policy, and Human Rights

*We must all accept the inevitability of ageing; what we do not have
to, and must not, accept is that old age brings with it lesser access to,
and enjoyment of, the full range of human rights.*

—Pillay, 2010

The world is getting older, with the population of people over the age of 65 continuing to surge. In 2012, 6% of the population in Africa was 60 years and older, compared with 10% in Latin America, 19% in North America, and 22% in Europe (U.N. Department of Economics and Social Affairs [UNDESA], 2011; Figure 9.1). However, the percentage of the aging population is increasing in the developing world, and by 2050 nearly 80% of people over the age of 60 will be in developing countries (unfpa.org/aging report). At the same time, the oldest old, those over the age of 80, is increasing most rapidly, with the number of centenarians projected to increase from fewer than 316,600 in 2011 to 3.2 million in 2050 (UNDESA, 2011).

These changing demographics have major implications as they impact both the economic and social structures of society. Income, employment, family, and retirement are among the key areas that are impacted by an aging population. Policy development in these areas remains a major challenge that often necessitates a major shift in resources and priorities.

FIGURE 9.1 Percent of population aged 65 and over: History and UN projection.

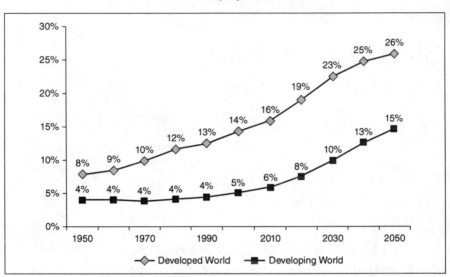

Source: UN (2005). Population Challenges and Development Goals, Department of Economic and Social Affairs, Population Division, UN

One of the foremost challenges that countries face with regard to aging is that of financial security. Both developed and developing nations are grappling with pensions and social security programs for this population, with almost all concerned about increased costs and diminished resources. Developed countries are dealing with the continued viability of pensions and benefits while developing countries often have no or very limited pension schemes to support retired persons. Consequently, without any retirement income, people must continue to work as long as possible. Without sustained pension schemes, poverty in old age becomes a reality.

Across the world, in both developed and developing countries, the family remains the primary source of assistance and support to older adults. But changes, such as increases in mobility and more women being employed, have impacted family support systems and caregivers who would traditionally have provided care are not necessarily available. Replacing or complementing these caregivers is a major policy concern. The issue is particularly critical in countries where there was a low birthrate, as there is often a dearth of adult children to provide care to older parents and parents-in-law.

Aging presents a challenge to health care systems, as there is an increased need for chronic care and rehabilitation services. Developing countries that are still dealing with infectious diseases may find it difficult to adequately care for the health care needs of older adults. Moreover, health professionals are not necessarily trained in understanding or treating the cognitive and functional impairments that can afflict older adults.

Many countries have recognized the need for policies that are congruent with the demands of an aging population. This chapter discusses the plans and policies of selected regions and countries with rapidly aging populations, all of which signed the Madrid International Plan of Action on Ageing (MIPAA). Particular attention is given to their implementation of human rights.

EUROPE

The United Nations Economic Commission on Aging (UNECA) established the Working Group on Aging (WGA) in 2008, which includes representatives from 50 European countries. The purpose of the WGA is to discuss aging policies and their implementation with regard to the MIPAA. It collects policy briefs and research briefs, monitors implementation, and assists in capacity development through training workshops and recommendations for aging plans (www.UNECE.org).

Sweden

Sweden invests more of its gross domestic products in its older population than any other country in the world, with its allocation being almost five times the average of other countries in the European Union (sweden.se/society/elderly-care-in-sweden/). Sweden also has one of the oldest populations in the world with 18% of its population over the age of 65 and a life expectancy of 79.1 years for men and 83.2 years for women.

The average retirement age in Sweden is 64, although between 2005 and 2011 the number of persons continuing to work increased by 49%. At retirement, people receive a national pension based on their income and the taxes they have paid, with an average monthly benefit of $1,748. Most people also receive an occupational pension based on contributions by their employer, although the majority, 65% of their total income, comes from the public pension system.

In April 2013, the government, concerned about a potentially large retired population and its burden on the pension system, released a report, *Measure for a Longer Working Life*, which focuses on ways to keep workers longer in employment. The report recommends a gradual increase in the retirement age. Among its other recommendations are changing the work environment so that it is adaptable to those with reduced capacities, combating age discrimination, offering older workers more opportunities for professional development, and educating them about the benefits of remaining in the workforce (Social Security, Sweden, 2013). Thus, as the report deals with economic concerns, it also reinforces many of the human rights of older adults with regard to employment.

Municipal grants and taxes fund most of the care for the older population, with a very small proportion (3%) financed by charges to older people. All health care costs to the elderly are subsidized with people able to choose whether to use private or public services to provide home assistance. The municipality is responsible for funding and allocating all services.

Policy focuses on enabling persons to remain in their own homes for as long as possible, with nursing homes used primarily for end-of-life care. Consequently, home help plays a major role in long-term care and provides the bulk of assistance to older adults requiring assistance, even those requiring 24-hour care. Each municipality sets its own rate for services depending on the type of care provided and the person's income. Municipalities also provide day care programs, meals programs, and transportation for those requiring it. Supportive housing is also under the auspices of the municipalities and is available for those needing more support and security. Admission is on a needs-assessment basis.

Municipalities are responsible for supporting the carers of older adults. Persons can receive payment either as a caregiver or as a cash allowance that assists them. However, with the state being the primary support provider for older adults, the dependence on families as caregivers is much less than in other countries.

The Swedish tradition of both federal and municipal responsibility for the older population with government funding has resulted in strong networks of public services supplemented with private programs. The rights of older adults are continually recognized through a commitment to a wide range of services, options, and supports that helps to maintain autonomy and independence in the community. Older adults, through their involvement in national and local pensioners' councils, also participate in the development of aging policy. The most recent policy is as follows:

Policy for Older People, Priorities for 2014 (Sweden Ministry of Health and Social Affairs, 2014)

1. Coordinated care for the elderly: Improving health and social care, increase cooperation between health and medical care and elderly care services.

2. Act on free choice systems: Increase opportunities for people to make their own decisions as to the providers of their services.

3. Continued focus on establishing a set of values: Services are to focus on enabling people to live their lives with dignity and a sense of well-being.

4. Support to family carers: Develop municipal supports for family carers.

5. Skills development: Strengthen skills of staff caring for older people.

6. Initiatives in housing: Develop sheltered housing and other elderly housing.

LATIN AMERICA

The population of Latin America and the Caribbean is aging more rapidly than in countries in the developed world. Although the population is very diverse, it is expected that by 2036 people over the age of 60 will outnumber children (U.N. Population Fund [UNFPA], 2012). The majority of older adults have no pension, and low social security benefits mean that many live in poverty. Families continue to play major roles in their support, but many struggle financially and their ability to assist is often limited.

Latin America has held several regional conferences on aging, which focus on implementing the MIPAA with a commitment to protect and promote the human rights and fundamental freedoms of all older people. Moreover, the constitutions of Venezuela, Brazil, Bolivia, Costa Rica, Columbia, the Dominican Republic, Honduras, Nicaragua, and Panama specifically state that older persons are entitled to special protection by the state.

In 2012, the Third Regional Intergovernmental Conference on Ageing and the Rights of Older Persons in Latin America was held in San Jose, Costa Rica. It generated the Charter on the Rights of Older Persons, with governments reaffirming their commitment to promote and protect the human rights and freedom of all older people. The countries also agreed to strengthen the right to social security and health while promoting independence, autonomy, and dignity (NGO Committee on Aging, 2012).

Several countries are working to foster older peoples' participation in policy development. Costa Rica, Chile, and Nicaragua established committees and councils that represent older persons and their organizations in national committees, while Uruguay, the Dominican Republic, and Peru hold consultations with older people in the drafting of their aging policies.

The region recognizes the concerns of an aging population and has taken steps through policies to address them. Although much more needs to be done, there is a definite recognition of both needs and rights of older persons. Moreover, by continuing to involve older adults in policy formation and by incorporating standards and the idea of rights of older persons into legislation, the countries are moving away from a needs-based to a human rights approach (Huenchuan & Rodriguez-Pinero, 2011).

Brazil

Brazil has the largest number of older people in Latin America, with almost 11% of its population over the age of 60 (UNDESA, 2011). Policies have continued to develop, beginning with the 1994 policy that guaranteed social rights by promoting autonomy, integration, and older adults' participation in society (Fernandes & Soares, 2012). Aging policy in 2003 had a more holistic approach by focusing on the interaction among physical and mental health, social status, and the freedom and dignity of older people, and also put in practice goals and targets of the Madrid Plan. In 2006, the National Conference of the Rights of the Elderly was held, which aimed to further guarantee the rights of older people.

The National Health Policy (2006) provides guidelines that encourage and support healthy aging. These include preserving their functional ability, autonomy, helping them to remain in the community, and improving their quality of life, including their social participation. The policy also called for further research on the elderly, increased health resources, improved access for medication, and a home hospitalization program (Fernandes & Soares, 2012).

The pension scheme in Brazil replaces 75% of a person's average income. Rural workers over age 60 and anyone over 65 who is poor can get a pension set at the minimum wage without having paid into the system. Social assistance benefits are given to elderly who do not qualify for pensions and cannot provide for themselves. However, with the population aging, Brazil faces the problem of how to continue to support these pension schemes (Queiroz & Figoli, 2012).

Older persons' participation in civil and social life has continued to increase through involvement in community-based social groups that encourage independence, productivity, and participation in civic activities. Data on the groups has found 20% of eligible seniors participating in 2002, increasing to 42% in 2010 (Benedetti, Orsi, Schwingel, Wojtek, & Chodzko, 2012). Participation also led to more engagement with other community groups and even reduced heath care costs.

Health care is a universal right and is provided by both public and private institutions through the Brazilian Unified Health System (SUS), with the elderly depending primarily on the public system. The health system is decentralized and health care delivery is the responsibility of municipalities that receive some support from state and federal governments. Home health care is developing throughout the country using teams of workers, and research indicates that when available, it is used (Thume, Facchini, Wyshak, & Campbell, 2011). There are few nursing homes or hospices and a severe shortage of geriatricians (Garcez-Leme & Leme, 2011).

The family provides much of the care to older persons, with most of these caregivers residing with them. However, there is no official policy that recognizes or supports family caregivers. Caregivers with low incomes may actually depend on the older person's pension for support. Presently, there are few resources of supports for caregivers.

Brazil is responding to the growth of its aging population through policies that reflect not just the needs of older people but also their rights. A more comprehensive pension system has been developed, changes have occurred in health care and participation of the elderly has increased. The government appears to recognize the importance of meeting the rights of older people through its policies that guarantee rights in accordance with the Madrid Plan.

A review of the impact of aging policies suggests that although progress has been made with regard to financial rights and pensions for older persons, less progress has been made with regard to their well-being and their social and human rights. Gaps in services continue to exist with little attention being paid to the supportive roles played by the family that impact the functioning and status of older people (Fernandes & Soares, 2012).

AFRICA

In 2010, 6% of Africa's population was over the age of 60; this will increase to 10% by 2050 (UNDESA, 2011). The majority of older people live in rural areas on barely subsistence incomes. In addition, HIV and AIDS have impacted many in the population; hence, traditional family structures and support systems have been decimated (UNFPA, 2011). Consequently, grandmothers are often responsible for raising orphans but receive little or no financial and other support services.

Households headed by the elderly are among the poorest on the continent, reflecting the poor status that people had throughout their lifetimes, as well as the absence of pensions (Nabalamba & Chikoko, 2011). Without employment, incomes, or land, many elderly, particularly older women, remain vulnerable. Lack of social services and supports, along with poor health care systems, is a stark reality in most countries. Moreover, as younger people have moved and become more socialized into modern society, traditional respect and support for older people has begun to wane (Nabalamba & Chikoko, 2011).

In 2002, the African Union Policy Framework and Plan of Action on Ageing offered a guide for the development of national aging policies including a focus on the rights of older people and the need for their participation in society. Since then, seven countries have developed national policies, but only Kenya, South Africa, and Tanzania have allocated budgets to these policies (UNFPA, 2011).

South Africa

In 2000, South Africa had the second highest number of older persons in Africa; this group is expected to grow more rapidly than those under 60 years of age, increasing at a rate four times higher than that of the population as a whole (Statistics South Africa, 2006). The Older Persons Act of 2006 focused on community care, the rights of older persons, protection of older persons, and residential care facilities to meet their continuing needs. Following recommendations of the Madrid Plan, the guiding principles were that older people should be able to live independently without fear of abuse and be treated fairly in the community. Among the goals were the development of a wide range of community-based services and programs, as well as training in gerontology and geriatrics. Older people would also be encouraged to participate in society and legislation, and primary and mental health care services developed.

A study by the South Africa Human Rights Commission (2010) found that access to health services was difficult, particularly for those in rural areas, with long waits in clinics. Residential care facilities were found to be substandard with poor regulation, abuse by staff, and poor funding (South Africa Human Rights Commission, 2010). Overall, the government does not give priority to the health of older adults but is focusing more on children. As an example, geriatric nurses have been shifted from the elderly to vaccinating children (Powell, 2013).

South Africa began offering a noncontributory old age pension in 1928. People over 60 are entitled to an older persons grant based on their income and assets, with a maximum benefit of approximately $135 per month and a small addition for those over 75 years (South Africa Government Services, 2014). In 2011, over 68% of the population between 65 and 69 years, and 77% of those 75–79, received the pension (Oosthuizen, 2012). Research indicates that the pension has reduced poverty among the elderly (Bhorat & Cassim, 2014).

As a result of HIV and AIDS, grandparents in South Africa have assumed major roles in raising orphaned grandchildren. Grandparents in South Africa have a legal duty to raise grandchildren whose parents have died. According to HelpAge International (2012), 40% of households are headed by older people raising an average of three orphans. Although they are entitled to a foster grant to assist them, these grandparents still face financial and social strains. Poverty is common among them; moreover, they also feel stigmatized and receive less community support than those caring for children who are not AIDS orphans (Kuo, Fitzgerald, Operario, & Casale, 2012).

Nongovernmental organizations (NGOs) are the primary means of older persons' participation in the community. They work to raise public awareness about policy issues and meet with ministers in the government about their concerns. However, although the overall perception is that older persons are frail and a burden and legislation has been passed that would support their rights, it has yet to be fully implemented (Powell, 2013).

ASIA

By 2050, one in four people in Asia will be over the age of 60, with a very high proportion being women (UNFPA and HelpAge International, 2012). These persons remain vulnerable to poverty, social isolation, and violence. Under the auspices of the United Nations Economic and Social Committee for Asia and the Pacific (ESCAP), the Asia-Pacific Intergovernmental meeting took place in Bangkok in 2012 to review countries' progress in implementing the Madrid Plan and exploring key priorities for action between 2013 and 2017 (United Nations ESCAP, 2013). Among the issues discussed were the rapid population aging, older women and gender discrimination, changes in the workforce and the risk of poverty in old age, family size and structure that impacts traditional support systems, care services and social security systems, and the need to create enabling environments for older adults who foster their right to participate in society. The conference also recognized the need for collection, compilation, and dissemination of data essential for further policy development.

A workshop on social integration and the rights of older persons was held in the fall of 2014 in Bangkok. The objectives were to exchange information on legislation related to the protection of the rights of older persons in the region, increase understanding about implementation and ways to address gaps, and initiate a dialogue among government representatives on how to best contribute to new practices (United Nations ESCAP Social Development in Asia and the Pacific, 2014). The results of the workshop are not available at the time of this writing.

Vietnam

Vietnam is rapidly aging, with older adults comprising 10.2% of the population. Due to family planning policies that limited the number of children and better health care, mortality rates in Vietnam have significantly decreased. The life expectancy at birth is 75.4 years and those reaching age 60 can expect to live another 18 to 20 years. Most of the elderly live in rural areas (UNFPA, 2011).

Family support of the elderly has been a tradition in Vietnam and is officially recognized in its 1992 aging plan that outlines the reciprocal responsibilities within the family of support for children and parents. Although most persons over 60 live with their children, the numbers have actually been decreasing, with a noticeable increase in those living with their spouse or living alone (UNFPA, 2011). Overall, there is a weakening in traditional support systems with a gradual replacement of the multigenerational family by nuclear families. Older women, those of advanced age, and those living in rural areas are particularly vulnerable to being without family support (Vietnam Women's Union, 2011).

The participation of older adults in society is perceived as an important aspect of policy making and is represented through the Vietnam Association of the Elderly (VAE), established in 1994, and the Vietnam National Committee on Aging (VNCA), established in 2005. Both groups receive some government support in their promotion and implementation of aging policies. Older people are involved in local associations, intergenerational self-help groups sponsored by VAE and HelpAge International, in which they discuss local policy concerns, advocate for change, and bring these issues to the attention of public officials (www.ngocentre.org, 2012).

The income of the elderly is lower than the national average and poverty rates are higher (UNFPA, 2011). The pension fund in Vietnam covers about 20% of the population, with the average benefit being about $152 per month and many receiving only $50. Consequently, a large proportion of the older population, particularly those living in rural areas who are less likely to have pensions, continue to work. At the age of 80, those with incomes below a specific level receive an additional $10 per month. Specific segments of the elderly population—women, ethnic minority elderly, and those in rural areas—have higher rates of poverty and are more likely to rely on families for financial support (Dzung, 2013).

Health care costs for those over age 60 are seven to nine times the cost for a child (UNFPA, 2011). Availability to health services is not uniform throughout the country and is particularly difficult for those in rural areas where there are few hospitals or community health centers. Accessibility to health care is limited, in that the individual is responsible for most of the cost with insurance playing a minor role. Health literacy among older adults is also very minimal and most do not understand conditions such as arthritis and hypertension. One of the activities of the intergenerational self-help groups is to provide more health education.

In 2010, the Ordinance of Older Persons was revised into the Law on the Elderly, which clearly stipulates the rights and responsibilities of society toward the aged. The law details obligations regarding care and older persons' roles as participants in society, prohibits age discrimination, and specifies the government's role in implementing the law. A study on the results of the first 2 years of implementation of the 2010 Law on the Elderly resulted in the following conclusions (VNCA and VAE, 2013):

1. Insufficient resources restricted the dissemination of the law and made it ineffective.
2. Health care for the elderly was still a major problem, particularly in remote areas.
3. Older adults had increased their participation in organizations and social activities with an increased understanding of their rights.
4. Poverty was being reduced in some localities but remained a problem.
5. Elderly contribute to their families through their employment and maintenance of traditions but also require more resources to increase their roles.
6. An absence of data on conditions of the elderly.
7. A decline in family care.
8. Concern that the present programs cannot meet future needs.

In summary, although much remains to be realized with regard to implementation of the law, the law itself and the government's continued interest in its aging population reflect an interest in meeting the needs and rights of older people. As can be observed in many countries, the overriding challenge is to make aging policy and services a government priority so that adequate funding is available for implementation.

AUSTRALIA

People aged 65 and older account for 13% of Australia's population, and projections are that this percentage will increase to 26% to 28% by 2051 (Australian Bureau of Statistics, 2008). Although there is no overall policy for older adults, support services in both the community and in residential settings are provided through various pieces of legislation. Australia also has an age discrimination commissioner whose role is to assure that the rights of older adults are recognized and supported.

The Aged Care Act of 1997 governs and licenses providers of both residential and home care, as well as provides access to services. Those seeking to use either government-subsidized residential or home care are assessed by the Aged Care Assessment Service, which determines eligibility based on physical, medical, psychological, and social needs. The National Aged Care Advocacy Program, a separate part of the Act, provides advocacy services for older adults through community-based organizations throughout the country and encourages their participation as advisors to the aging agenda.

The National Aged Care Package of 2010 has the responsibility of providing home- and community-based care, increasing incentives for general practitioners to provide more services for older persons in care homes and expanding services in rural communities. The government also instituted a single entry point for aged care services so that access to the system is easier. Australia focuses on integrated housing for older adults, with the provider arranging and delivering support and care services to the residents. Rent assistance is available in these communities to those with incomes that are insufficient to cover the rents.

In 2013, the Living Longer Living Better aged care reform package, a 10-year plan, was passed. It gave priority to providing more support and care at home, better access to residential care, and more support for persons with dementia; it also strengthened the aged care workforce (Australian Government, 2014). Various aspects of the package include increased support to carers who provide most of the assistance to older adults, reforms to provide easier access to services, counseling, and respite care. Carer support centers were established in July 2014 as places where the aged could go for assistance and emergency respite. Carers, based on their income and assets, are also eligible for carer payments that help with care if the person is unable to work because of the care he or she provides. A carer's allowance, which is not income or asset related, is offered to those providing daily care to someone who is frail or disabled.

Both home care and consumer-directed care continue to develop. The country offers four levels of home-care packages, ranging from those for persons needing help with only basic needs to those with more complex needs. Consumer-directed care intends to give consumers greater control over the services as well as the providers. Beginning in 2015, all home care will be delivered through consumer-directed care packages.

The Living Longer Living Better reform also recognizes the needs of older Australians with diverse backgrounds. Within the program is a strategy for lesbian, gay, bisexual, transgender, and intersex (LGBTI) seniors. The strategy was developed in consultation with organizations representing these populations and is focused on assuring that services are accessible and sensitive to their particular needs. The diverse backgrounds area also includes a strategy for meeting the needs of those from culturally and linguistically diverse (CALD) backgrounds.

Employers are required to contribute 12% to employee retirement accounts, to which employees can also contribute. Age Pension, a public program, is available for those over 65 who meet income and asset tests. The pension is noncontributory and paid from public funds. To encourage people to remain in the workforce past retirement age, a work bonus is offered that increases the amount they can earn before having their pension reduced. The maximum payment in 2014 was $15,544 for a single person and $29,437 for a couple. With the expected aging of the population, the pension eligibility age is set to increase to 67 in 2023. With the anticipated costs that the system will make on the government, there are also recommendations for raising the retirement age to 60 and raising the asset level (Barnett, 2014).

Dementia was recognized as a national priority in 2005. Dementia Collaborative Research Centers were established to conduct research on the disease and carers. The National Framework for Action on Dementia 2013–2017 provides priorities for policy, such as workforce, education, research, diverse needs, environment, and community. Health reforms also include residential care for people with dementia, and improvement in hospital and primary care.

Australia continues to focus on its aging population through the development of several policies associated with the main concerns of older adults. The policies also reflect many of the human rights principles associated with security, independence, and well-being. By encouraging and supporting advocacy, older adults are participating in developing aging agenda and remaining integrated in the community assuming a social capital role.

SUMMARY

The countries and their policies described in this chapter highlight the ways in which older adults are impacting society. Each of the countries discussed has developed policies to meet the needs of their older citizens with varying recognition and emphasis on their human rights. The policies of each reflect underlying sociocultural and economic factors and the ways in which aging and the aged are perceived in their society. These in turn appear to affect the resources available to older adults as well as their rights and ability to live fulfilling and independent lives.

Meeting the economic challenge of an older population along with changes in family structures requires planning and policies in several areas. Pensions, accessible health care, family assistance, housing and community services, and formal support programs that can assist older adults in their homes are among the areas where reforms are most needed. But, these programs have yet to be fully developed, meaning that older adults remain vulnerable. Only one-third of all countries have comprehensive social protection schemes, most of which cover only those in formal employment (UNFPA and HelpAge International, 2012). With a considerable number of older people in developing countries having spent years working in agriculture or in jobs not covered by pensions, these workers are denied these basic pensions and thus face years of poverty.

The right to the highest possible standard of health remains a challenge in developing countries. Access remains limited, particularly in rural areas and places where resources to expand services for the elderly are not a priority. Specialists and long-term care facilities are rare, and there is a noticeable absence of mental health services in most countries.

One area in which the rights of older adults appear to be supported is in their participation in communities and in policy development. Through local associations and NGOs, they are encouraged to become involved in both networks and with the government. Such participation is important for their own empowerment, for increasing their integration, and for combating discrimination.

The countries discussed thus far have plans for addressing the needs of an aging population and all recognize the importance of human rights. Implementing policies to address the needs and rights of older adults does not necessarily require more resources. It depends upon political commitment that perceives these policies as a priority. Until this occurs, only token efforts to meet the concerns of an aging population can be expected and existing policies will remain vacuous. In addition, there is a noticeable absence of human rights indicators or benchmarks. Without sufficient data, it is impossible to know how effective existing programs are in meeting either needs or rights.

Of the countries reviewed, Sweden and Australia are the most committed to implementing comprehensive policies that address both needs and rights of older adults. Both countries are aware of the economic and social demands placed by an aging population and both are focusing on responding to them. They have incorporated priorities of the Madrid Plan as directions for policy implementation, which are (1) integrating older persons in the development process so that they are assets rather than burdens, (2) supporting healthy aging and economic well-being in old age, and (3) promoting enabling and supportive environments for older adults. Although the resources of Sweden and Australia surpass those of developing countries, their plans and their implementation may serve as models for improving the lives and well-being of older adults.

QUESTIONS FOR DISCUSSION

1. Describe some of the major global concerns associated with aging populations and ways in which they relate to human rights.
2. Explain which of the aspects of Sweden's policies with regard to aging you would like to see adapted by other countries.

3. Describe the ways in which the countries are encouraging the participation of older adults in the community. Why is this important?

4. Give examples of how countries have integrated needs with human rights into their aging policies.

REFERENCES

Australian Bureau of Statistics. (2008). *Australian historical population statistics.* Retrieved from http://abs.dov.au/AUSSTATS/abs@nsf/Lookup

Australian Government. (2014). *Living longer. Living better.* Retrieved from http://www.livinglongerlivingbetter.gov.au/

Barnett, A. (2014). *The age pension in Australia, past, present, and future.* Retrieved from http://learn.nab.com.au/the-age-pension-in-australia-past-present-and-future

Benedetti, T. R. B., d'Orsi, E., Schwingel, A., & Chodzko-Zajko, W.J. (2012). Convivência Groups: Building active and healthy communities of older adults in Brazil. *Journal of Aging Research,* 612–918. doi:10.1155/2012/612918

Bhorat, H., & Cassim, K. (2014). *South Africa's welfare success story II: Poverty reducing social grants.* Retrieved from http://www.brookings.edu/blogs/africa-in-focus/posts/2014/01/27-south-africa-welfare-poverty-bhorat

BRASIL. Ministério da Saude. Secretaria de Vigilância em Saúde. Política Nacional de Promoção da Saúde. Brasilia, DF,. 2006. Disponível: http://portal.saude.gov.br/portal/arquivos/pdf/Politica_nacional_%20saude_nv.pdf. Acesso: 20 agosto, 2006

Dzung, N. (2013). *Elderly people in Vietnam: Some issues of concern from a family and gender perspective.* Retrieved from http://aassrec20th.files.wordpress.com/2013/04/ngo-thi-tuandung-paper_final.pdf

Fernandes, M., & Soares, S. (2012). *The development of public policies for elderly care in Brazil.* Retrieved from http://www.ee.usp.br/reeusp/

Garcez-Leme, L., & Leme, N. (2011). *Costs of elderly health care in Brazil: Challenges and strategies. Medical Express.* Retrieved from http://medicalexpress.net.br/details/36/Costs-of-elderly-health-care-in-Brazil-challenges-and-strategies1

HelpAge International. (2012). *South Africa.* Retrieved from http://www.helpage.org/where-we-work/africa/south-africa/

Huenchuan, L. & Rodriguez-Pinero, L. (2011). *Ageing and the protection of human rights: Current situation and outlook.* New York, United Nations: Economic Commission for Latin America and the Caribbean.

Kuo, C., Fitzgerald, J., Operario, C., & Casale, M. (2012). Social support disparities for caregivers of AIDS-orphaned children in South Africa. *Journal of Community Psychology, 40,* 631–644.

Ministry of Health and Social Affairs. (2014). *Sweden.* Retrieved from http://www.regeringen

Nabalamba, A., & Chikoko, M. (2011). *Aging population challenges in Africa.* Retrieved from http://www.afdb.org/fileadmin/uploads/afdb/ Documents/Publications/Aging%20Population%20Challenges%20in%20 Africa-distribution.pdf

NGO Committee on Aging. (2012). *San Jose Charter on the Rights of Older Persons in Latin America and the Caribbean.* Retrieved from http://www.ngocoa-ny. org/events/regional-conferences/san-jose-charter-on-the.htmlon.edu/ papers/110746

Oosthuizen, M. (2012). *South Africa's state old age pension.* Retrieved from http://www.ipc-undp.org/conference/south-south-learning-event/ presentations/Morne%20Oosthuizen.pdf

Pillay, N. (2010). *International Day of Older Persons, 1 October 2010.* Retrieved from www.ohchr.org/en/NewsEvents/Pages/DisplayNews.aspx?NewsID= 10402&LangID

Powell, A. (2013). *Mandela's care spotlights S. Africa healthcare needs for elderly.* Voice of America, June 20.

Queiroz, B., & Figoli, M. (2012). *The social protection system for the elderly in Brazil.* Retrieved from http://paa2011.princeton.edu/papers/110746

Social Security, Sweden. (2013). Retrieved from http://www.socialsecurity. gov/policy/docs/progdesc/intl_update/2013-05/index.html#sweden

South Africa Government Services. (2014). *Older persons grant.* Retrieved from http://www.services.gov.za/services/content/Home/ServicesForPeople/ Socialbenefits/oldagegrant/en_ZA

South Africa Human Rights Commission. (2010). *Seventh economic and social rights report 2006–2009.* Cape Town: Author.

Statistics South Africa. (2006). Retrieved from http://www.statssa.gov.za/ census01/Census/Database/

Thume, E., Facchini, L., Wyshak, G., & Campbell, P. (2011). The utilization of home care by the elderly in Brazil's primary health care system. *American Journal of Public Health, 101,* 868–874.

United Nations, Department of Economic and Social Affairs. (2011). *World population ageing: Profiles of ageing 2011*. Geneva: United Nations.

United Nations, Department of Economic and Social Affairs. (2005). *Population challenges and development goals, percent of population 65 and older: History and UN Projection*, United Nations, NY

United Nations, Department of Economic and Social Affairs. (2013). *Report of the Sixth Asian and Pacific population conference*. Retrieved from http://www.unescapsdd.org/files/documents/PUB_APPC6-Report-20140403.pdf

United Nations Population Fund (UNFPA). (2011). *Ageing in Vietnam*. Retrieved from http://vietnam.unfpa.org/webdav/site/vietnam/shared/Publications%202011/Ageing%20report_ENG_FINAL_27.07.pdf

United Nations Population Fund (UNFPA) and HelpAge International. (2012). *Ageing in the twenty-first century: A celebration and a challenge*. Geneva: United Nations Population Fund.

Vietnam National Committee on Aging (VNCA) and Vietnam Association of the Elderly (VAE). (2013). *Assessment on implementation of the Law on the Elderly in VietNam*. Hanoi: Authors.

Vietnam Women's Union. (2011). *Viet Nam aging survey, 2011*. Key findings. Hanoi: Women's Publishing House.

CHAPTER 10

Policy Challenges in Meeting the Rights of Older Adults

A post-2015 development agenda should account for a progressively and rapidly ageing world by promoting healthy ageing and economic well-being in old age and by providing enabling and supportive environments where older people are integrated into the development process as an asset rather than a burden.

—UN System Task Team, 2012

Such integration as that described in the opening quotation would recognize and integrate older adults as social capital within society. Policies that promote social ties, social networks, activities, and the involvement of older adults in communities would simultaneously combat isolation and age discrimination and benefit society as a whole. Concomitantly, the social capital perspective, with its focus on participation, may also further substantiate the rights of older adults in the community. As stated by Doron and Apler (2010), it is not old age that makes certain rights hard to enjoy, but a particular notion of old age that denies the full enjoyment of rights to the aging.

Older adults are younger adults with additional years. They are not a separate population group. Even so, discrimination based on age remains prevalent throughout the world. Discrimination marginalizes and disenfranchises older adults, and in doing so treats them as a problem to be solved rather than as equal members of the community who are entitled to the same basic human rights. Often shrouded in beneficence and best interests, ageist attitudes can override the right of an older adult to his or her autonomy and independence. Ageist attitudes themselves contribute to dependence as they further separate and discriminate against older adults. The challenge is to combat discrimination by assuring that age is not treated as a proxy for a person's value, ability, or worth. Doing so is critical for assuring that rights are met and that older people are able to live with respect and dignity.

Within the United States, as in many countries, varying policies address the needs of older people but do not treat them as rights. The result is needs-based policies, with those in power determining what these needs are and their priority. Such needs and the problems are seldom associated with human rights and the role of the duty bearers, those in power, to fulfill them. Moreover, without recognition of such rights, their indivisibility can easily be ignored with focus given to one area such as health, while income or security is ignored. Moreover, as policies continue to differentiate between groups, the rights of some remain highly at risk.

Integrating older adults and engaging them in society is a first step to combating discrimination and providing a basis for rights-based policies. Political participation itself is a right under the Universal Declaration of Human Rights (UNDHR) (Article 21) and is central to the position of right-holders in society. Direct and informed participation of older persons in the design of public policy is central to their integration as right-holders (U.N. Office of the High Commissioner for Human Rights [UNOHCHR], 2014). Unfortunately, although essential, mechanisms to ensure older adults' participation are generally inconsistent, nonexistent, or weak.

Empowering older adults by encouraging them to actively participate in society helps to combat ageism, while it also develops social capital. Through advocating and networking, engaging older adults as experts in their own lives, as knowledgeable, and as contributing partners in society increases their inclusion and thus substantiates their roles as full participants in society. Such engagement also helps to counteract perceptions of dependency that contribute to age discrimination. The challenge is assuring that older adults are engaged and involved and thus can play the dual roles of duty-bearers and right-holders.

In the United States, the Older Americans Act defines participation as "an individual or collective action designed to address a public concern or an unmet human, educational, health care, environmental, or public safety need" (U.S. Administration on Aging, 2006). Accordingly, the White House Conference on Aging brings together thousands of older adults and others from across the country to help formulate policies for the coming decade. The participation of these persons is key to the development of resolutions that lay the foundation for future legislation and polices.

The importance of the participation of older adults in the development of policy is further underscored in WHO's report on age-friendly communities (WHO, 2007). The report recommends that older adults assume key informant and advisory roles on policies to ensure their involvement in community decisions that impact them. As discussed in this book, Sweden, Brazil, and Vietnam are examples of countries that have made particular efforts to engage older adults, through local associations, in policy development.

The right to social security (Article 22, UNDHR) and the right to a standard of living adequate for well-being (Article 25, UNDHR) are threatened as older adults remain vulnerable to poverty. Without sufficient assets or pensions, retirement becomes a period of financial struggle that leads to dependency. The need for a basic minimum income for older adults is a major global challenge. In more developed countries, financial crises can impact both private and public pensions with the result being decreases in benefits. In less-developed countries, persons are often not covered by a pension or receive insufficient benefits and thus have no financial security in their later years of life.

Social Security is the primary source of income for most older Americans and is particularly important for minorities, older women, and those who have had lifetimes of low earnings (AARP, 2013). However, it is these very groups who are most likely to be poor. Thus, although Social Security has reduced the overall number of persons living in poverty, many still struggle to live on inadequate benefits that impact their quality of life. Having contributed to the system throughout their working years, they are still unable to achieve a financially secure retirement.

Pension plans associated with employment can play important roles in keeping older adults out of poverty. Unfortunately, the same groups—minorities, women, and less-skilled workers—who are at risk for low Social Security benefits are most at risk of not receiving retirement pensions. Moreover, the continued decline in both public and private pensions, particularly those offering defined benefits, as well as the inability of many corporations and municipalities to meet financial obligations means that many older adults with such plans encounter financial insecurity in retirement. The challenges in the United States, as well as in many other countries, is to strengthen pension plans so that they remain a source of financial security at retirement and to increase the participation of groups that have traditionally been left out of programs.

The right to employment (Article 23, UNDHR) is often challenged, as age discrimination is common within the workplace. Even with laws in force to protect them, older adults are vulnerable to unequal treatment by employers with regard to training and often face a greater risk of being laid off. Once unemployed, older adults are at risk of long-term unemployment, which further impacts their financial security. Combating workplace ageism by underscoring the contributions of older workers, assuring that they participate in training programs, and making the workplace more amenable to them would benefit both employees and employers. Moreover, helping to maintain older adults in the workforce can have a pronounced impact on society as they continue to contribute to rather than draw upon both Social Security plans and pensions.

The aging of the workforce also means greater risk of having employees with some level of ADRD. The rights of these persons can be severely threatened as their abilities and strengths are overlooked with the focus being on their impairment. The challenge is to assure that the strengths and abilities of these employees are engaged as long as possible and that employers are given the needed training to engage, work with, and support them.

Everyone has a right to "life, liberty, and security of person" (Article 2, UNDHR). The importance of this right cannot be underestimated as older adults prefer to remain in their own homes, aging securely in place, within their communities as long as possible. However, doing so poses a challenge for those who support them and have insufficient resources. Assistive technology that can enable people to remain in their homes even with impairments remains expensive, with little public financing to assist with cost.

The need for accessible and supportive housing far outweighs its availability, and funding has not kept pace with the demand. Continuing care communities and assisted-living facilities which could enable many to remain in the community are unaffordable for the majority of older adults. Both the villages and naturally occurring retirement communities (NORCs) offer models that include strong engagement ties, volunteers, and mutual assistance to older adults in the community. The challenges are to further replicate and expand on these models so that they are available and accessible to more groups of older adults.

There is no greater challenge to security and liberty than guardianship, which curtails an individual's right to independence and autonomy. Improving guardianship procedures, including assessments and monitoring, is critical to safeguard the rights of older adults. Standardizing regulations and accountability are prerequisites for assuring that it does protect the interests and well-being of older adults. Until regulations are strengthened, the risk for abuse and the welfare of many older adults in such programs remains high.

Families continue to be the major sources of support for older adults in most countries. However, the ability of families to provide assistance has become limited due to various factors, such as mobility, caregivers who are employed, and the increasing care demands that often accompany aging. Over the years, there have been countless studies on the strains and burdens that family caregivers encounter, and yet, there is an overall absence of policies that would financially assist them and offer them support. Moreover, existing policies remain underfunded and are limited in scope and effectiveness. Consequently, within the United States caregivers must often choose between providing care for an older adult and assuring their own future financial security. Recognizing the major role that families play in the lives of older adults and developing policies and services that support them is critical and yet remains a challenge in most countries.

Long-term care remains a major challenge in the United States and in many other countries. As populations continue to age, the risk of chronic conditions that impede functioning and the need for supportive services increases. However, aging policy in the United States remains fragmented, with underdeveloped community services and supports that are often supported with inadequate funds and resources. The majority of the burden of care continues to fall on unpaid informal caregivers who frequently struggle to deal with increasing burdens. The Medicare program continues to focus on acute rather than chronic care and thus fails to address the health care needs of many older adults. With limits on home care, hospital care, and nursing home stays, many older adults who pay privately are at risk of not receiving needed care. Medicaid assistance that provides more comprehensive coverage is not available to many who are outside of its income parameters, while cuts in funding to Medicaid programs may result in service reductions.

The challenge is to create a comprehensive long-term care policy that would provide an array of services accessible to all needing assistance. Strengthening home-based and community care programs, which can reduce the need for and bias toward institutionalization while permitting older adults to remain in the community as long as possible, is essential for advancing the health, security, and well-being of older adults. Shifting from the current needs-based to a rights-based system of long-term care would support autonomy and the dignity of many older adults.

Older women throughout the world are perhaps the most vulnerable group. Across the globe, women outlive men, and for most these later years are ones of struggle (United Nations, 2012). The cumulative inequality that results from lifetimes of lower incomes, less participation in pension plans, and often less power and ability to fully participate in society severely impacts their well-being. Women are the most likely group to spend their last years alone, dependent upon others for support, in poverty, and with few resources. Only by removing barriers that continue to segregate them throughout their lives can some measure of equality be achieved in their later years.

Combating elder abuse, whose victims are primarily women, remains a challenge across the globe. As the population continues to age, increasing numbers of older adults, particularly women, will be at risk of being abused or neglected. It is a complex issue with many risk factors and thus demands many types of interventions. Although the problem is recognized in the United States and policies and programs have been enacted to tackle it, their effectiveness is restricted by limited funding. The challenge is to recognize the extent of abuse, neglect, and exploitation and provide sufficient resources to enforce policies that can combat it.

The overall and perhaps greatest challenge in all countries is to assure that discrimination is replaced by integration and that older adults are considered and treated as full members of society. When this occurs, age will no longer be a proxy for competency and inclusion, and human rights may be realized. As long as older adults are marginalized and perceived as a burden, these rights remain at risk. Involving them as duty-bearers through their participation in policy making and the government, as well as rights-holders, is critical for integration. Rather than being perceived and treated as dependent, they can assume the roles of actors in policy formation. Accordingly, the challenge is to move from a needs-based perspective of aging policy to one based on rights.

Access to services, health care, employment, and an adequate income and support can help to ensure that older adults continue to age with dignity and independence. Without resources that sustain and promote such access, older adults remain vulnerable and their rights obscured. Without question, aging is often accompanied by declining health, but accessible health care and long-term care services can help many to remain autonomous and live full lives.

Moreover, as the quality of life for older adults is closely correlated with the resources and advantages that they had in their earlier years, combatting poverty and inequality throughout the life span, redressing social imbalances is fundamental to achieving social justice and rights in the later years.

Older adults, just like younger adults, are not a homogenous population. Diversity requires sensitive policies that reflect such differences as those associated with gender, sexuality, and even immigrant status. Policies that exclude these groups from full participation in their younger years continue into the later stages of life with rights continually threatened.

Indicators and benchmarks that can serve as tools that measure progress toward human rights are seldom utilized. Programs such as those under the AOA collect data on participation and service utilization but are difficult to interpret in relation to rights. Moreover, the involvement of older adults, the rights-holders, in developing these indicators is questionable. Qualitative measures that assess older adults' perceptions of staff or programs would augment these data as they may record attitudes of rights-holders regarding programs, the extent to which they felt that objectives were met, and even how they might be improved. Developing such uniform indicators and collecting the data are often time-consuming and costly, but doing so would certainly reflect a social commitment to achieving the rights of older adults.

At the global level, a Convention on the Rights of Older Persons under the United Nations would provide global recognition to their vulnerability and specific concerns and the role of governments in addressing them. When a country ratifies a convention, it becomes obligated to respect the principles and rights that it entails. Countries must provide periodic reports on their policies with respect to the principles and standards of the covenant. Special rapporteurs may also investigate a country to ascertain whether violations are occurring and explore ways of rectifying them, with countries being made responsible for appearing before the United Nations Monitoring Committee to explain their positions and policies.

Thus, a convention offers the promise of stronger adherence to guaranteeing the rights of older adults. To date, the United Nations has passed only the Principles for the Older Person (1999), which emphasizes that attention be given to older persons in certain areas but does not mandate specific policies to meet them. A Convention on the Rights of Older Persons would help to assure that countries develop legal frameworks that detail and make these rights binding. The need for a convention has been stressed by the Human Rights Chief of the United Nations, Navi Pillay: "Human rights of older persons have depended upon an international legal regime that is fragmented, uneven, and incomplete and there must be a particular focus on ageism and age discrimination along with participation, access to an adequate standard of living, employment, and health" (Office of the High Commissioner for Human Rights, 2014).

Finally, there is global recognition that the population is aging. Longer life expectancies and declining fertility rates will continue, resulting in new social and economic changes requiring new responsive policies. Many countries, including the United States, have developed policies that address the concerns of an aging population, but in most instances these are focused on needs rather than rights. Thus, they tend to be treated as problems that must be resolved rather than rights that might be fulfilled. Changing the perception to rights is critical as it creates the foundation from which advocates and those impacted can act (Fredvang & Biggs, 2012).

To date, there are many existing policies associated with aging, and problems and goals have been identified, but implementation often remains weak as the policies are given little priority. The global recession has had a major impact on economies that has affected older adults' employment and pensions, impairing their rights. At the same time, many countries have readjusted budgets with less funding for programs that could benefit older adults. Resources necessary to enact policies and put them into practice must compete with other political and social concerns. Without actual implementation, rights cannot be fulfilled.

Social policy is often distinct from, rather than integrated from, human rights. Nowhere is this more evident than in policies for older adults in which needs rather than rights tend to dominate. As long as age remains a discriminatory factor, a proxy for impairment, problems, and dysfunction, needs rather than rights will continue to dominate in the policy arena. Perhaps a key to changing this perspective would be the recognition that older adults will actually be us in time and that ensuring "their" human rights ensures our own.

All human rights are indivisible and pertain to everyone, regardless of age. As long as the rights of older adults are overlooked, their concerns given little priority, and their participation in society marginalized, both they and society suffer. Regardless of age, people can contribute to society; when they are no longer able to do so, they are entitled to financial and other support that enable them to live with dignity and security. Policies that confirm and protect these rights are the hall-mark of a just society.

QUESTIONS FOR DISCUSSION

1. In your view, what do you see as the first priority that countries should focus on in assuring the rights of older adults?
2. Why should anyone care about the rights of older adults?
3. Do you believe that a UN convention on the rights of older people is necessary? How might it impact their rights?
4. How might empowerment of older adults impact aging policy? What can be done to foster their empowerment?

REFERENCES

AARP. (2013). *Sources of income for older Americans, 2012.* Public Policy Institute. Washington, DC: AARP.

Doron, I., & Apter, I. (2010). The debate around the need for a new convention on the rights of older persons. *The Gerontologist, 50,* 583–593.

Fredvang, M., & Biggs, S. (2012). *The rights of older persons: Protection and gaps under human rights law.* Social Policy Working Paper, No. 16. Melbourne: Brotherhood of Saint Lawrence and University of Melbourne Centre for Public Policy.

U.N. Office of the High Commissioner for Human Rights. (2014). *UN human rights chief offers her support for a new Convention on the Rights of Older Persons.* Retrieved from http://www.ohchr.org/EN/NewsEvents/Pages/RightsOfOlderPersons.aspx

U.N. System Task Team on the Post-2015 UN Development Agenda. (2012). *Population dynamics* (May). New York: United Nations.

United Nations. (2012). *Current status of older persons.* Retrieved from http://www.un.org/esa/socdev/ageing/documents/publications/current-status-older-persons.pdf

U.S. Administration on Aging. (2006). *H.R. 6197—109th Congress: Older Americans Act Amendments of 2006.* Retrieved from http://www.aoa.gov/AoA_programs/OAA/oaa.aspx

World Health Organization (WHO). (2007). *Global age friendly cities: A guide.* Geneva: Author.

The Universal Declaration of Human Rights

On December 10, 1948, the General Assembly of the United Nations adopted and proclaimed the Universal Declaration of Human Rights, which is presented here.

PREAMBLE

Whereas recognition of the inherent dignity and of the equal and inalienable rights of all members of the human family is the foundation of freedom, justice and peace in the world,

Whereas disregard and contempt for human rights have resulted in barbarous acts which have outraged the conscience of mankind, and the advent of a world in which human beings shall enjoy freedom of speech and belief and freedom from fear and want has been proclaimed as the highest aspiration of the common people,

Whereas it is essential, if man is not to be compelled to have recourse, as a last resort, to rebellion against tyranny and oppression, that human rights should be protected by the rule of law,

Whereas it is essential to promote the development of friendly relations between nations,

Whereas the peoples of the United Nations have in the Charter reaffirmed their faith in fundamental human rights, in the dignity and worth of the human person and in the equal rights of men and women and have determined to promote social progress and better standards of life in larger freedom,

Whereas Member States have pledged themselves to achieve, in cooperation with the United Nations, the promotion of universal respect for and observance of human rights and fundamental freedoms,

Whereas a common understanding of these rights and freedoms is of the greatest importance for the full realization of this pledge,

Now, therefore, The General Assembly, Proclaims this Universal Declaration of Human Rights as a common standard of achievement for all peoples and all nations, to the end that every individual and every organ of society, keeping this Declaration constantly in mind, shall strive by teaching and education to promote respect for these rights and freedoms and by progressive measures, national and international, to secure their universal and effective recognition and observance, both among the peoples of Member States themselves and among the peoples of territories under their jurisdiction.

ARTICLE 1

All human beings are born free and equal in dignity and rights. They are endowed with reason and conscience and should act toward one another in a spirit of brotherhood.

ARTICLE 2

Everyone is entitled to all the rights and freedoms set forth in this Declaration, without distinction of any kind, such as race, color, sex, language, religion, political or other opinion, national or social origin, property, birth or other status. Furthermore, no distinction shall be made on the basis of the political, jurisdictional or international status of the country or territory to which a person belongs, whether it be independent, trust, non-self-governing or under any other limitation of sovereignty.

ARTICLE 3

Everyone has the right to life, liberty, and security of person.

ARTICLE 4

No one shall be held in slavery or servitude; slavery and the slave trade shall be prohibited in all their forms.

ARTICLE 5

No one shall be subjected to torture or to cruel, inhuman, or degrading treatment or punishment.

ARTICLE 6

Everyone has the right to recognition everywhere as a person before the law.

ARTICLE 7

All are equal before the law and are entitled without any discrimination to equal protection of the law. All are entitled to equal protection against any discrimination in violation of this Declaration and against any incitement to such discrimination.

ARTICLE 8

Everyone has the right to an effective remedy by the competent national tribunals for acts violating the fundamental rights granted him by the constitution or by law.

ARTICLE 9

No one shall be subjected to arbitrary arrest, detention, or exile.

ARTICLE 10

Everyone is entitled in full equality to a fair and public hearing by an independent and impartial tribunal, in the determination of his rights and obligations and of any criminal charge against him.

ARTICLE 11

1. Everyone charged with a penal offence has the right to be presumed innocent until proved guilty according to law in a public trial at which he has had all the guarantees necessary for his defense.
2. No one shall be held guilty of any penal offence on account of any act or omission which did not constitute a penal offence, under national or international law, at the time when it was committed. Nor shall a heavier penalty be imposed than the one that was applicable at the time the penal offence was committed.

ARTICLE 12

No one shall be subjected to arbitrary interference with his privacy, family, home, or correspondence, nor to attacks upon his honor and reputation. Everyone has the right to the protection of the law against such interference or attacks.

ARTICLE 13

1. Everyone has the right to freedom of movement and residence within the borders of each State.
2. Everyone has the right to leave any country, including his own, and to return to his country.

ARTICLE 14

1. Everyone has the right to seek and to enjoy in other countries asylum from persecution.

2. This right may not be invoked in the case of prosecutions genuinely arising from nonpolitical crimes or from acts contrary to the purposes and principles of the United Nations.

ARTICLE 15

1. Everyone has the right to a nationality.
2. No one shall be arbitrarily deprived of his nationality nor denied the right to change his nationality.

ARTICLE 16

1. Men and women of full age, without any limitation due to race, nationality, or religion, have the right to marry and to found a family. They are entitled to equal rights as to marriage, during marriage, and at its dissolution.
2. Marriage shall be entered into only with the free and full consent of the intending spouses.
3. The family is the natural and fundamental group unit of society and is entitled to protection by society and the State.

ARTICLE 17

1. Everyone has the right to own property alone as well as in association with others.
2. No one shall be arbitrarily deprived of his property.

ARTICLE 18

Everyone has the right to freedom of thought, conscience, and religion; this right includes freedom to change his religion or belief, and freedom, either alone or in community with others and in public or private, to manifest this religion or belief in teaching, practice, worship, and observance.

ARTICLE 19

Everyone has the right to freedom of opinion and expression; this right includes freedom to hold opinions without interference and to seek, receive, and impart information and ideas through any media and regardless of frontiers.

ARTICLE 20

1. Everyone has the right to freedom of peaceful assembly and association.
2. No one may be compelled to belong to an association.

ARTICLE 21

1. Everyone has the right to take part in the government of his country, directly or through freely chosen representatives.
2. Everyone has the right to equal access to public service in his country.
3. The will of the people shall be the basis of the authority of government; this will shall be expressed in periodic and genuine elections which shall be by universal and equal suffrage and shall be held by secret vote or by equivalent free voting procedures.

ARTICLE 22

Everyone, as a member of society, has the right to social security and is entitled to realization, through national effort and international cooperation and in accordance with the organization and resources of each State, of the economic, social, and cultural rights indispensable for his dignity and the free development of his personality.

ARTICLE 23

1. Everyone has the right to work, to free choice of employment, to just and favorable conditions of work and to protection against unemployment.
2. Everyone, without any discrimination, has the right to equal pay for equal work.
3. Everyone who works has the right to just and favorable remuneration ensuring for himself and his family an existence worthy of human dignity, and supplemented, if necessary, by other means of social protection.
4. Everyone has the right to form and to join trade unions for the protection of his interests.

ARTICLE 24

Everyone has the right to rest and leisure, including reasonable limitation of working hours and periodic holidays with pay.

ARTICLE 25

1. Everyone has the right to a standard of living adequate for the health and well-being of himself and of his family, including food, clothing, housing and medical care, and necessary social services, and the right to security in the event of unemployment, sickness, disability, widowhood, old age, or other lack of livelihood in circumstances beyond his control.
2. Motherhood and childhood are entitled to special care and assistance. All children, whether born in or out of wedlock, shall enjoy the same social protection.

ARTICLE 26

1. Everyone has the right to education. Education shall be free, at least in the elementary and fundamental stages. Elementary education shall be compulsory. Technical and professional education shall be made generally available and higher education shall be equally accessible to all on the basis of merit.

2. Education shall be directed to the full development of the human personality and to the strengthening of respect for human rights and fundamental freedoms. It shall promote understanding, tolerance, and friendship among all nations, racial, or religious groups, and shall further the activities of the United Nations for the maintenance of peace.

3. Parents have a prior right to choose the kind of education that shall be given to their children.

ARTICLE 27

1. Everyone has the right freely to participate in the cultural life of the community, to enjoy the arts, and to share in scientific advancement and its benefits.

2. Everyone has the right to the protection of the moral and material interests resulting from any scientific, literary, or artistic production of which he is the author.

ARTICLE 28

Everyone is entitled to a social and international order in which the rights and freedoms set forth in this Declaration can be fully realized.

ARTICLE 29

1. Everyone has duties to the community in which alone the free and full development of his personality is possible.

2. In the exercise of his rights and freedoms, everyone shall be subject only to such limitations as are determined by law solely for the purpose of securing due recognition and respect for the rights and freedoms of others and of meeting the just requirements of morality, public order, and the general welfare in a democratic society.

3. These rights and freedoms may in no case be exercised contrary to the purposes and principles of the United Nations.

ARTICLE 30

Nothing in this Declaration may be interpreted as implying for any State, group, or person any right to engage in any activity or to perform any act aimed at the destruction of any of the rights and freedoms set forth herein.

Index